Where We Learn
Reimagining Educational Spaces

FRAME

Contents

Introduction

Education is the future or said differently, there is no future without learning. But as we don't know the future, education must adapt to every moment of contemporary life, respond and propose something new: a vision of the future. Hence in the proposition for education, two opposites meet. While the exact outcome of the future is uncertain, our vision and understanding of the present are brought to the fore within ideological and architectural structures that propose certainty. Adapting how we learn is the only way to learn something genuinely new.

In 2022, we know that our current situation is not promising. As a population, we face unprecedented planetary, political and social challenges that require immediate action. To harvest our time's technological and creative potential, we need to leave the straight-jacketed and strict paradigms once associated with a fruitful education behind and allow space for experimentation, inclusivity and expression. Expressing the hunger of multiple generations to change the world for the better, the spaces in which we learn are rapidly adapting to become radical yet fluid containers for the production and the sharing of knowledge, exactly how and where it is needed the most.

This book explores 43 projects at the forefront of this movement, picking up the four fundamental notions we have identified to drive the new spaces in which we learn. Accordingly, the book is organised into four chapters – Designing with Agility, Innovation, Community and Nature. Naturally, many of these projects respond to more than one driver. Reading the key takeaways of each chapter clarifies why that is a success and how they can be integrated when approaching a project with an education scope. The most important feature of the projects presented here is their diversity, arguing powerfully that there is no single way but a cacophony of possibilities and needs that include learning for multiple ages; learning in urban and rural settings; learning in solitude and community and learning in ways and spaces that have not been seen before.

What effect will these spaces have on our future and that of generations to come? We don't know with certainty, but we know that a different future is possible. We know that change can be learned. We hope that readers will be inspired by the courage of the architects included in this volume and find practical references to take and expand upon in their own spaces and communities.

DESIGN

6

WITH
AGILITY

7

A. Lerman Architects breaks open a residential area's dense horizon with the TEO Center for Culture, Art and Content, an enclave for art and creativity overlooking the vast ocean

RIGHT In this densely populated residential area, the flat layout of TEO Center for Culture, Art and Content stands out and creates a feeling of spaciousness, accessibility and calm.
Photo A. Lerman Architects

HERZLIYA The Theodor Herzl Center for Culture, Art and Content stands in such stark contrast with the area in and for which it has been built that its purpose becomes immediately evident. Communicating openness among the privacy of luxurious mansions and tall housing developments in the district of Herzliya, north of Tel Aviv, the low-rise complex exposes itself with a vast panorama toward the ocean.

A breath of freshness and simplicity lies over TEO's modernist structure, assembled from prefabricated and site-cast concrete elements within a 50 x 50 m² plan set around a central patio. The various programmes and functions of the public cultural centre extend to a music conservatory, a dance school, an art and ceramics studio, a gallery, a senior recreation centre and a cafeteria. Connection, community and multidisciplinary expertise are fostered in the unique cultural facility, making it a focal point for the knowledge exchange between the city's art practitioners and residents. A partially inserted upper floor completes the offer with a library and a 300-m² open deck for gatherings and activities. For as much as an architectural intervention can be a functional statement with immediate social impact, TEO's success lies in the inversion of the city's urban fabric and the creation of a nodal point that unites various types of learning in the public sphere.

ABOVE Concrete units – partly cast on-site and partly precast – unite with textured glass and metal in a unique geometric shape that strongly defines all exterior and interior surfaces.

RIGHT The central patio connects the various spaces creating a safe internal area for gatherings.
Photos Amit Geron

TEO CENTER FOR CULTURE,
ART AND CONTENT

A. LERMAN ARCHITECTS   11

TEO CENTER FOR CULTURE,
ART AND CONTENT

PREVIOUS SPREAD Large window panels give luminosity and transparency, inviting users of the building to see each other and connect from afar.
Photo Nimrod Levi

ABOVE Layers of concrete panels and minimal architectural intervention shine a light on the purpose of the building, which acts as a display box for cultural activities and works.
Photo Amit Geron

RIGHT TOP Various functions can be hosted in the bright studio spaces, ranging from painting and ceramics to dance and cultural events.
Photo Nimrod Levi

RIGHT BOTTOM Creating a public gallery space was central to TEO's mission to connect the cultural centre to the existing urban fabric and tease visitors to come in.
Photo Nimrod Levi

The building breaks open the horizon, offering learners a vision to share

TEO CENTER FOR CULTURE,
ART AND CONTENT

In an important heritage site destined for tourism, a2o architecten and AAC Architecture inspire the next generation to learn how past and future coexist at Straf! KABO Beringen

STRAF! KABO BERINGEN

BERINGEN In Flanders' largest industrial heritage site, tribute is being paid to the region's mining past across 100,000 m² of existing building heritage. What makes Beringen unique in Europe is that the industrial heart of the mine has been preserved to be redeveloped as a mix between heritage, recreation and tourism with urban functions such as living, working and shopping – giving the mining land, once dedicated to the extraction, a dignified, valuable and contemporary interpretation.

In this setting, the former bathing halls of the complex have been converted into a nursery and an elementary school with after-school care. Physically and symbolically, the past and the future communicate here. The existing facades of the building have been kept while new additions have been placed in a retained manner that does not impose itself but lets history breathe. Wooden elements, large windows and minimal design interventions in toned colours function as a framing device, highlighting the stylistic features of the existing building in plain sight rather than imposing themselves to transform it. The design reflects the school's philosophy, which follows a strong focus on living learning in all its activities, allowing children to discover their surroundings playfully.

ABOVE The ground floor is an open plateau made of a large concrete slab, which rests on robust beams and columns.

RIGHT The colossal building once served as a storage unit for mine wagons and provided changing rooms for the miners. The renovation has left the aesthetic of the heritage-listed structure intact while adapting it to new functions.

Architectural features that bring the existing heritage into the future without imposing itself on them

LEFT The new materials contrast warm and cold while creating a tranquil atmosphere and an understated context in which the original patina comes to the fore.

BELOW The nursery school has eleven classrooms and a reception room, which brings young learners together to help them build social skills and play.

LEFT TOP Lively details like the blue play house are intended to break the sober minimalism of the overall design.

LEFT BOTTOM Despite creating sixteen classrooms for the primary school, there's still a seeming excess of space and generous open plan areas the architects have preserved.

RIGHT Overpowering clarity and gentle contrast are continuous elements of the applied methodology, warm materials that mingle with more sterile elements.

A1.21

Aurora Arquitectos spells it out with ARTAVE/CCM Music School: here comes the sun

RIGHT The bright addition acts as a connection between two existing blocks of classrooms while overlooking an outdoor amphitheatre.
Photos Aurora Arquitectos

ABOVE The vibrant yellow volume brings a radical and stark contrast against the architecture of the school's buildings.

RIGHT The indoor area remains consistent with the exterior's warm, sun-themed colour scheme.

CALDAS DA SAÚDE A strange volume in vibrant yellow, consequent all the way through, extends and links the buildings of the ARTAVE/CCM Music School in Caldas da Saúde, located a few kilometres from Porto. The goal was to break away from the stratified architectural expression of the existing buildings after various interventions on the structures. Rather than adapting to any of the styles, the new volume is an act of radical novelty. It sneaks into the space between adjacent buildings, leaving their individuality intact while taking its own space to shine.

     With vertical and horizontal connections for the school areas, Aurora Arquitectos designs new student meeting spaces and a brutalist outdoor amphitheatre for joint meetings. On the inside, the use of yellow continues in more orange hues. Other areas are left distinctly to contrast with black and white features, such as the graphical terrazzo floor. The surrounding small forest lends the building a happy tropicality and vividness, contagious among pupils and visitors. Windows are placed to frame the views, while the corrugated steel panels, naturally yellow, are the perfect backdrop for the lush chlorophyll-filled leaves.

Designed and built in record time, <u>Jinlong School</u> by <u>Crossboundaries</u> is out to solve real-world problems

RIGHT Aerial view of Jinlong School with the industrial surroundings of Shenzhen's Pingshan district. The visible dormitory facade comprises different prefab panels, with large-scale public spaces highlighted by yellow cut-outs.
Photos Qingshan Wu

SHENZHEN Responding to the government's mission to balance rapid population expansion and an overall shortage of public schools in the Chinese metropolis, Crossboundaries developed the 36-classroom Jinlong School and its campus. The appeal of the challenge is twofold: first, to be as creative as possible to manage the limitations in budget, timing and a tiny site area of roughly 16,000 m². Second, the mandatory use of prefabricated components and metal composite elements that, at the same time, provide a functional solution to a problem that will become more pressing in cities around the world shortly.

Notably, the required efficiency in construction has been paired with an attention to creating a distinctive aesthetic quality and attention to people-oriented spatial relationships. To avoid the monotony of colour or size, six different prefabricated panels have been used to make space for variation in an overall unified facade. Public spaces, which account for roughly one fourth of the area, have been built using traditional construction methods to avoid repetitiveness or a sense of oppression. Special consideration was given to the sports fields, which are not in the periphery of the campus but lie at its very heart: the running track has been built on a platform in the central courtyard, allowing space below for other sports areas, art, library and multifunctional rooms.

LEFT Prefabricated panels in different thicknesses and colour hues are applied at the dormitory facade, from the most protruding coloured in light grey to the less protruding in dark grey. Balconies behind evenly distributed openings allow for more depth in the appearance of the surface.

RIGHT Taking the subtropical climate of Shenzhen into account, the circulation areas remain open. Perforated panelling is used for the handrails revealing movements behind.

BELOW Pathway to the lower level, the cross-connection of the campus which links the educational and residential quarters.

Grafton Architects promise a light-flooded workspace to the <u>Town House, Kingston University London</u>

LONDON Universities are notoriously complex places to design. The list of needs and desires is extended, while the typology of required spaces is often contradictory. The idea of an open-plan layout competes with the need for dedicated and specialised work environments, tranquillity and intimacy that fosters community.

Inside the new Town House, part of Kingston University London, the architects imagined reading, dance, performance, lectures, exhibitions, research and learning to coexist within the same space, proposing the juxtaposition of physically active and contemplative activities to make the area live. More than half of the entire project was required to be open-plan by the brief, including a barrier-free open-door policy toward passers-by and the local community.

The primary design concept follows the classical tradition of the 'portico', a porch leading to the entrance of a building, or extended as a colonnade, with a roof structure over a walkway, supported by columns or enclosed by walls – emphasising a primary frontal relationship with this most public thoroughfare connecting to Kingston Town Centre, stretching along the entire 200-m length of the university frontage to Penrhyn Road. External terraces, walkways and balconies are elevated above the street, vines feature on the west facade, and a series of stepped roof gardens with green and brown roof technology has been installed to integrate landscaping.

ABOVE The seating possibilities that extend around the central atrium are manifold and give sight to more learning spaces on the other floors, letting each others' presence inspire students.

RIGHT Interlocking spaces bring different students together and connect various expert spaces to break into the communal territory.

The Check Point Building for the Faculty of Computer Sciences at Tel Aviv University by Kimmel Eshkolot Architects is the technological innovation it claims to be

BELOW Light-flooded and with
windows onto the adjacent garden
is how the university wanted to
accommodate students in the new
building.

RIGHT A central atrium connects
all the floors and learning spaces
via shared balconies, creating
a sense of unity and visual
interconnectedness.

NEXT SPREAD With a small
intervention, functional spaces
like stairs and hallways become
meeting points that facilitate social
interaction casually.

TEL AVIV Located in the centre of the Tel Aviv University campus, the Check Point Building is a new technology-integrated building with a unique envelope made of pixels of glass designed using parametric modelling. The new computer sciences faculty distinguishes itself by having a structure principally based on the same innovative technology it sets out to further research, teach and develop with students. 'Technology often inspires architects and enables the realisation of ideas which were not possible in the past. In the Check Point Building, technology no longer merely serves the architecture, but has become an essential part of the architectural idea,' says Etan Kimmel of Kimmel Eshkolot Architects.

The development of the unique technology that gave shape to the building, named after cyber security cooperation Check Point, was one of the determining factors of the result. Clad in pixel-like glass panels of various types measuring 40 x 40 cm, the envelope offers multiple levels of transparency and reflectivity that respond according to the needs of the indoors' users – transparency in the windows and garden areas and sealing in other parts.

Flow and movement continue to be leading principles on the inside, where the classrooms are centred around a central atrium, whereas the staircase accompanies students through a sequence of spaces that flow out into co-working areas.

It appears to be constantly changing, from material to reflection, blending with the sky and clouds

THE CHECK POINT BUILDING FOR THE FACULTY OF
COMPUTER SCIENCES AT TEL AVIV UNIVERSITY

Conceived by <u>Max Arkitekter</u> and <u>Caroline Olsson Arkitektur</u>, the early exercises in decision-making at <u>Bobergsskolan</u> prepare the pupils of the school for what's to come after

BOBERGSSKOLAN

ABOVE Even in shared facilities, unique nooks and hideaway places that offer intimacy and tranquillity have been created to respond to different energy levels and introversive moments.

LEFT Transparency and connectivity dominate architectural features, giving children an overview while teaching them trust and security.

STOCKHOLM A school for 900 students has been fitted in and placed in an old industrial environment, Ferdinand Boberg's gasworks in Hjorthagen. The project brief demanded the new school be in line with the existing complex yet unmistakably contemporary.

As a whole, the school is made of four volumes which include an old workshop and connect with each other below the ground floor. The buildings adopted the structure of the gasworks, their simple shape and the gable motifs, and the brick ornamentation of its facades. Apart from its large size, it is a rich experience to move through the indoor spaces of the school – they appear to be a never-ending series of colourful backgrounds. The materials and the colour palette used to speak of a different context and target group, which is part of what the architects set out to achieve: bringing a holistic, rich and sophisticated architecture to children.

Designed as a socially sustainable school, Bobergsskolan places particular demands on security, belonging and extra care that oscillates between giving students of different ages clearly separated spaces in the building body while allowing for spatial openness and meeting places for exchange. Transparency and connectivity between other storeys and galleries give pupils a sense of control and security, giving children an overview and a sense of agency from which to make decisions.

The architecture invites pupils to be curious and get an overview of where they are and which route to take, preparing them instinctively for the art of decision making

ABOVE No difference has been made between play and life, potentially any moment, and any circumstance in this building accommodates children and invites them to be playful.

RIGHT TOP There is specific attention to sustainability in all facilities that the school accommodates, giving pupils a direct example and educating their vision and senses towards natural products.

RIGHT BOTTOM Nothing is boring here, not even the reading room. Bright colours and inventive shapes entice young learners to engage with them.

<u>Xaverius College Kindergarten Borgerhout</u> does the doable within a residential area of town thanks to <u>META</u> architectuurbureau

RIGHT Responding to an urgent need in a dense residential area, the school is designed to fit in on the only available lots between already existing buildings in the neighbourhood.
Photos Filip Dujardin

ABOVE The long L-shaped form extends over one floor only. This way, toddlers do not need to take flights of stairs and can meet all together in the communal garden.

RIGHT TOP Indoor spaces are characterised by simplicity and functionality that can be adapted to necessity.

RIGHT BOTTOM The long corridor allows pupils to mingle and know where to find each other with ease.

NEXT SPREAD The kindergarten entrance sits comfortably between two existing buildings of the neighbourhood. Greenery gives space to breathe.

ANTWERP To tackle a lack of space inside the existing school, Xaverius College embarked on the practical mission to purchase various lots within a residential area. The patchwork of different plots and buildings was demolished to make space for a sombre, L-shaped layout that comes to define the new kindergarten now.

The story and architecture are unassuming and straightforward, born out of a concrete necessity and expected with a sense of tranquil urgency. This new project doesn't pretend to propose a reform of pedagogical design. 'And that's probably the strength of this project. Due to its typology, it brings education to what it needs to be. Nothing more. Nothing less,' so explain the architects.

META designed an L-shaped volume that has one level to prevent toddlers from having to climb unnecessary stairs. The heart of the building is conceived as a long, covered walkway connecting all the spaces. While it offers room for supporting functions, such as a cloakroom, toilet facilities and storage rooms, its primary function is to flood the pairs of classrooms with natural light coming from openings toward several courtyard gardens. Offering school space precisely in the neighbourhood where it was needed, this school perfectly fulfils its function.

XAVERIUS COLLEGE KINDERGARTEN
BORGERHOUT

META ARCHITECTUURBUREAU 51

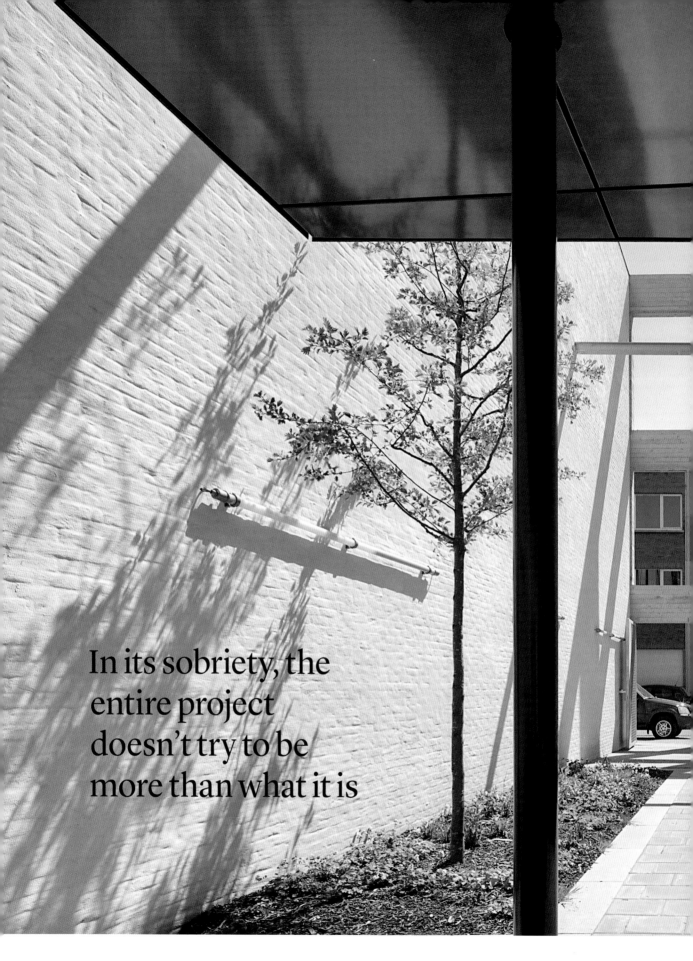

In its sobriety, the entire project doesn't try to be more than what it is

Light and space are the main ingredients coming together at the Integrated Secondary School Mahlsdorf designed by NKBAK

INTEGRATED SECONDARY SCHOOL
MAHLSDORF

ABOVE Modular structure with large window panels that give each classroom a panoramic view.

RIGHT After aluminium cladding on the outside, the inside exposes warm timber units which run through the entire building.

BERLIN 'Designing and building a school is always something special: it does not want to show under what financial, bureaucratic and administrative conditions public school buildings have to emerge. And it wants to convey a sense of openness, clarity, sovereign stability and clever wisdom to the students and teachers.' With the ambitious dedication of integrity, the architects approach the idea of creating a school environment.

In Mahlsdorf, situated in the eastern suburb of Berlin, the task has been solved with a large, elongated meandering structure seemingly made from windows alone. The generosity and simple shapes form the indoor spaces. A central entrance hall is the heart piece from which wide corridors extend, offering a bright and light atmosphere. Colour-contrasting recreation areas make it easy to find and offer identity together with the likewise coloured stairwells.

Defined by economic efficiency, the three-storey school building was designed as a modular wooden structure with a flat attic roof, prefabricated and assembled on site. A second main characteristic of the building is its environmental sustainability. This includes using ecological building materials produced with low energy consumption and whose recycling allows an enabling circularity. Materials that bind carbon dioxide or are made in a resource-saving way were the preferred choice, intended to create an ecological awareness among the future pupils and strengthen the relationship to natural materials.

ABOVE Using modular timber construction has had a significant advantage in time and took less than 6 months from start to finish.

LEFT The colourful interior modules highlight specific areas and reflect through the adjacent walls.

All usable spaces
are defined by
large, openable
window facades

DESIGN WITH AGILITY

In Rocco Design Architects Associates' iADC Design Museum, design, form and function agree to non-conformism

ABOVE Different lighting conditions meet in and around the folded facade to give it character and define the building.

RIGHT Large concrete columns support the grandeur of the entrance and frame the staircase, which can be used as an outdoor showcase and introduction to the design expositions.

SHENZHEN Situated at the heart of the Shapu Art District in Bao'an, the art district took an experimental urban planning approach resulting in the use of art and culture as the main driver of the city's development. The iADC Design Museum positions itself as one of the significant cultural establishments to weave layers of identities into a new man-made district.

Within the area, the museum itself is a floating volume creating an urban threshold plaza. It encourages urban interactions by connecting with the adjacent facilities within the community. Devoted to contemporary design, the museum aims to act as a platform linking international and local designers through exhibitions, symposiums and lectures inside its various gathering spaces – multiple galleries, an exhibition hall, an auditorium, a cafe and more.

Starting with a pure box structure, the museum is transformed with one simple act: folding its facade, breaking the formal rigidity and giving the building a vibrant and free-spirited ambience. On a symbolic level, it is an expression of openness that signifies an unleashing of creative energy from its status quo. Inside the museum, the galleries are spatially arranged around a central courtyard which admits daylight into the space. The folded facade further enhances the experience by filtering natural light between the gaps, reducing the need for artificial lighting and minimising energy consumption.

The folded facade is the highlight of the exterior and functions as a symbolic framing and light regulator

LEFT Geometric variations of the cube are found throughout the building's interior.

RIGHT TOP The colour scheme is limited to variations of grey and white, giving the centre stage to the varying artworks on display.

RIGHT BOTTOM The austere character of the minimal design is contrasted by the warm and extensive placement of light.

<u>TEMP</u> proposes <u>X Museum Beijing,</u> an art museum that breaks with the art world minimalism

RIGHT Among the many contemporary art museums in China, the X Museum differentiates itself for its architecture, its focus on emerging Chinese artists and its young founders.
Photos Jin Weiqi

ABOVE The letter X is the main symbol of the museum and adorns the entrance in the form of an intersection of two H-beams supporting each other structurally. The large roof underneath is perforated to filter patterns of light.

RIGHT TOP Infinity mirrors and steel details give the interior a feeling reminiscent of *The Matrix*.

RIGHT BOTTOM The interior charms with grey rounded wall cladding that also serves as support for installing artworks.

BEIJING If the Berlin art scene is shaped by leather and latex, the material of choice in Beijing seems to be metal. X Museum Beijing is clad in a matrix of 54 steel boxes with protruded rectilinear structures that throw an array of shadows onto the posterior grey stucco wall – angle and length are constantly changing with changes in natural light.

The facade prepares visitors for what is to follow inside, where more metal and corrugated steel walls negate any expectation of the white cube concept. Instead, a more flexible, colourful and modular approach has been chosen with custom-made terracotta bricks extruded with horizontal slots that allow metal clips to hang artwork. It is a system capable of supporting different mediums and works of art while responding to the constantly evolving contemporary art scene with a spatial reflection and a halt. Although the white cube must be filled and reimagined each time to guarantee the corresponding form of arrangement and installation, the mode of coming into relation with work and its structure is predefined and thus narrower. After all, it is a well-proven fact that limitations increase creativity.

The diagram of the X composed of two lines is signified as the most basic form of interaction

Key takeaways

1 Identifying and delivering educational spaces exactly where they are needed is paramount. There are quasi-natural inbuilt imbalances in urban textures that propagate and lead to peripheries deprived of cultural or community areas and metropolitan areas not providing schooling facilities. To counterbalance them, architects must act with extreme agility to provide the residents in question with what currently lacks.

2 Finding creative solutions regarding materials, building in a modular manner or reusing existing buildings to create innovation out of the lack of space, time and funding.

3 A mindset determined to be flexible is needed to resist the polarisation between densely populated and deserted areas and tailor an architecture that withstands such categories to offer livelihood. Apart from a close collaboration with the authorities, the residents and close familiarisation with the physical environment, a solid capacity to adapt and act fast is beneficial to go beyond the limitations imposed by the situation.

DESIGN

72

FOR
INNOVATION

73

As <u>Aybars Aşçı</u> underlines, empathy is an important concept in learning environments and creating an architecture of connections is at the heart of the <u>Avenues Shenzhen Early Learning Center</u>

AVENUES SHENZHEN EARLY LEARNING
CENTER

AYBARS AŞÇI (EFFICIENCY LAB
FOR ARCHITECTURE)   75

PREVIOUS SPREAD The new elevated walkways bridge across public roads, connecting the campus building and creating a safe pedestrian circulation network. The bridges meander among existing Banyan trees, offering a unique path of travel.
Photo Si Hu

ABOVE A hybrid of urban infrastructure and play structure, vertical playgrounds descend from the bridge, forming a rooftop treehouse that weaves through the trees. The bridge immerses students in the lush surrounding environment.
Photo Si Hu

RIGHT New slab openings are cut into the original concrete frame to facilitate new visual connections and multi-level atria inside the Early Learning Center.
Photo Zhang Chao

SHENZHEN Repurposing seven existing buildings of the urban village, the design team created a campus master plan that responds to various needs simultaneously. On the one hand, it minimises the carbon footprint of new construction by reusing already available building complexes. On the other hand, it responds perfectly and, one could argue, in much more imaginative ways than most purpose-built schools, to the needs and desires pupils might have.

The buildings are connected by a network of elevated walkways and bridges, creating a myriad web of roofscapes with outdoor learning spaces and gardens. It's an entire concept based on connection: physical connections that offer an interweaved network of pedestrian walkways, carefully choreographed visual references and the connection to nature. But most importantly, the spaces are functional while being surprising and diverse, from tropical green bridges among banyan trees to bright indoor spaces with innovative glass blackboard surfaces that offer moments of discovery, encouraging exploratory learning and teaching children a healthy and natural approach to the use of space.

AVENUES SHENZHEN EARLY LEARNING
CENTER

AYBARS AŞÇI (EFFICIENCY LAB
FOR ARCHITECTURE)   79

The different design scenarios provide a colourful playground from which to learn about life

PREVIOUS SPREAD Glazed walls act as an interactive surface on which children can draw and creatively learn.

LEFT The principal of 'connections', be it physical or visual, is carried out throughout the Center by the use of colours and strategically placed atriums and openings.

RIGHT TOP Large windows within the classrooms flood the learning spaces with natural sunlight.

RIGHT BOTTOM Diagonal views are provided by the cut-out and orchestrated atria.

Photos Zhang Chao

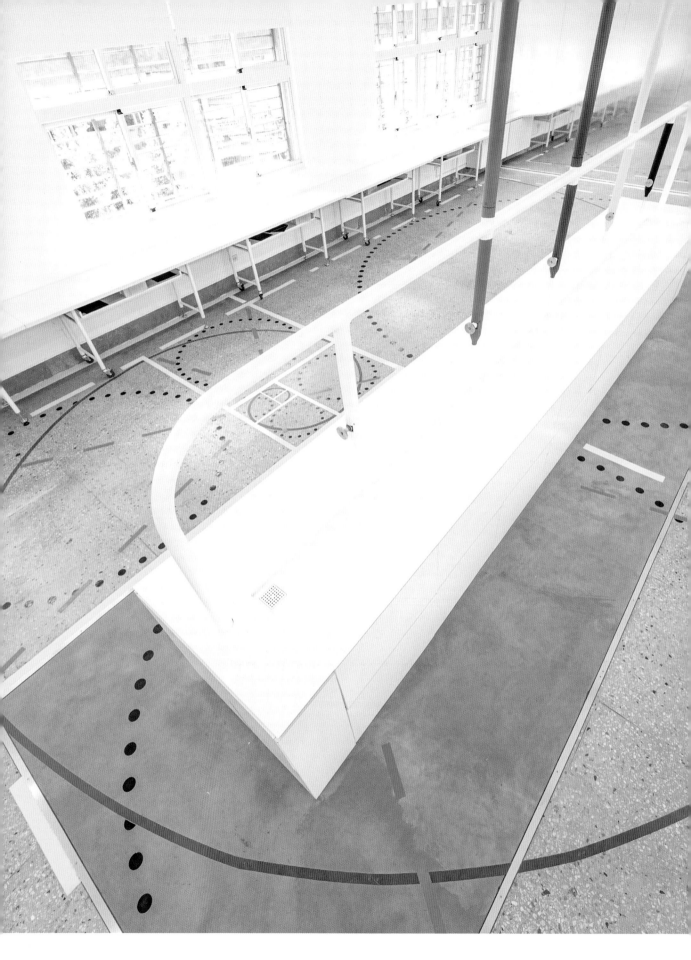

Aesthetic Lab is a receptacle for the chemical reaction between rational knowledge and perceptual imagination by CloudForm Laboratory

ABOVE The purpose of the centralized storage unit is to free up the remaining space for the users by maximizing the usage area. Everything around it becomes optional; even tables and chairs can be removed entirely if not needed.

RIGHT TOP Detail of the colourful water faucets.

RIGHT BOTTOM The integrated storage unit organises away every form of clutter.

TAIPEI A space as white as one might imagine the parody of an Apple advertisement. In the futuristic classroom, everything has been reduced to white, sleek and minimal surfaces to leave room for the imagination of the young students that can configure the space each day anew. The modular design maximises space by making a central island the only fixed element in the room, integrating water faucets, outlets, storage space and other functions in the centre of the classroom with bright colours that flow down from the ceiling. Tables are moveable, and chairs can be folded to accommodate diverse teaching functions and communicate visually that each day is a new day. Things can be made and made again in a different way, constantly.

The spatial hierarchy introduced by a traditional blackboard has been broken. Instead, the entire front wall of the classroom is a whiteboard, while the back wall features a gradual mirror to simulate the transition between the real and the imagined. It is a classroom that is supposed to function as a framing device rather than a space that imposes anything. An exciting feature adopted from art schools in the provision of exhibition space: the central island's platform can be used to display projects at semester-end exhibitions, wherein students can replace the ceiling's rail-mounted lights with projection lights to illuminate the fruit of their labour.

Imbued with intelligent features, the spartan room favours discovery and initiative

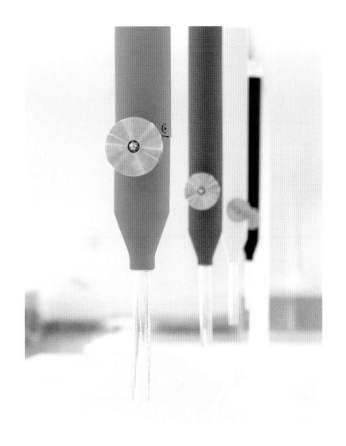

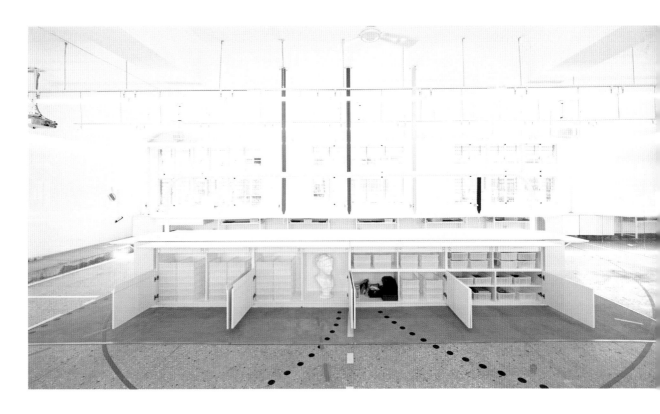

Industrial renovation by <u>Kokaistudios</u>: first step in the <u>Baoshan WTE Exhibition Center</u> within a 'green park city'

RIGHT One of the site's few factory buildings has been transformed into an Exhibition Center and functions as a symbolic gateway to this landmark scheme. **Photos** Terrence Zhang

ABOVE A mix of nature, industrial remnants and clever architecture create a magic atmosphere around the complex.

RIGHT No matter how rough, all architectural elements come together to support the main protagonists: the light and the industrial outdoors.

SHANGHAI In a uniquely iconic site, the renovation realised by Kokaistudios brings together a derelict industrial site, all its grit and signs of intense usage, with the neat contrast of minimal architectural intervention.

The specificity of the site lies precisely in highlighting this relationship between the old and the new rather than hiding it or cleaning it up. The industrial memory stays intact here, accentuated by prefabricated elements and reusable materials that speak of a different time. In a straightforward construction process of only 4 months, the architects have succeeded in installing a sanctuary to exhibit models, drawings and plans outlining the broader development of the site, playing an essential educational role through hosting students studying green energy strategies.

Through a well-considered dialogue between light and heavy materials, translucent and solid, dirty and clean, the exhibition centre brings to the fore the need for a new ecological context and future to be considered. Touching the strings of its visitors and collaborators already when they look at the site for the first time creates an emotional connection and situation of direct physical understanding of an abstract and complex issue.

The soft poetry of the architectural intervention gives the educational component its force, as an urgent invitation rather than a dragging need

Co-learning, co-creating, co-working is the collaborative model realised in ksestudio's Afterschool Learning Hubs 1 & 2

DESIGN FOR INNOVATION

AFTERSCHOOL LEARNING HUBS 1 & 2

ABOVE Simple but powerful: powdery mint green and complementary orange line the space with bright highlights that bounce off each other in different shapes and objects.

LEFT Bright colours frame the entire project and imbue the rigid geometry of the place with life.

NEXT SPREAD A brutalist playground but with colour, this is where teenagers come to work and learn.

CHALCIS Afterschool Learning Hubs 1 & 2 are both unusual spaces, offering independent and group learning settings to learners of varying ages. Learning Hub 1 follows the logic of a co-working space where the mantra is defined by the possibility of being together yet alone and having the ability to realise absolutely anything that might be necessary during the school day – regardless of a video call, a group meeting, silent study, making coffee or preparing a meal, taking a breath of fresh air, printing a document or relaxing for a moment. This list could effortlessly become longer and, at second sight, clarifies that such multifaceted, flexible spaces are usually not offered to younger age groups or anyone outside of the logic of work. Yet, here it is, colourful, varied and simple.

Learning Hub 2, focusing on younger learners, produces a series of teaching nooks both indoors and outdoors. Classes can be held in the courtyard, on the steps, on the rooftop, in the lobby and in the classrooms. Accents of colour and light are scattered throughout the learning spaces to promote interaction and communication.

In both hubs, playfulness and colour are the keys to this experience, as is the possibility to meet others, strangers even, who are engaged in other activities and allow for a meeting that responds directly to the building design: an opportunity to immerse oneself in a different world for a brief moment, a moment that might change one's perspective.

ABOVE Colour is a continuous feature of the structure, giving value to every space and making it a potential spot for informal meetings or hangouts.

RIGHT The small kitchenette provides a separate space marked by dusty blue and serves as a meeting point between classes.

The playfulness of the design gently stimulates learners to try different settings while offering them the fulfilment of all their needs

With <u>The Youth Activity Center</u>, Beijing enjoys a space dedicated to developments yet to come by <u>Moguang Studio</u> and <u>REDe Architects</u>

RIGHT Abstract geometric components are found throughout the site, comprising landscape design and a central playground at the centre of the various buildings. **PHOTOS** Zhi Xia

THE YOUTH ACTIVITY CENTER

ABOVE The original industrial site in Beizhuang Town, Miyun District, comprised a dozen disused buildings arranged around two courtyards and surrounded by factories and mountains, which have been transformed.

RIGHT TOP The building facades are embellished with geometric color blocks and lines, with a view to evoking kids' imagination and stimulating them to interact and explore the distinctive venue.

RIGHT BOTTOM The abandoned canteen in the factory has been transformed into the hostel's reception hall. The design strategy of combining exquisite artistry with the mottled texture of the internal surface in the existing building allows the new and old elements to coexist harmoniously without compromising their authenticity.

BEIJING It is lucky to get to work with a site like this. Initially, a garment manufacturing factory of 5000 m², the young architects tasked with the renovation into a youth education camp decided to keep the original structure of the factory complex. Their holistic approach wasn't focused on single buildings. Still, keeping intact the spatial narrative weaved into the building over time, the original walls and the relationships between different parts of the complex while creating an ambitious program of classrooms, a restaurant, a conference room and accommodation. Gardens and landscape facilities function as connectors between different programs, such as the activity space of the northern courtyard to the accommodation area of the southern yard.

Moments of contained playfulness pierce the severe renovation project, for example, the red steel platform, which invites children to play and run while providing shading for activities on the lawn. While recycled red bricks and cement are used throughout for hard paving, plastic running tracks are rolled out for children to run, jump and have fun. The choice of materials has been carefully considered, the paving mainly uses recycled bricks and stones from the old buildings demolished around the site, and the structural materials are primarily steel, avoiding the use of concrete and other materials in large quantities. It has the air of a project for the future: a space that has been imbued with a vital mission and leaves empty room to grow.

Blurring the existing landscape, architecture and installation, the project transforms into a mix of imagination and remembrance

Nomoto Sekkei proposes a unique aesthetic language to teach the engineers of tomorrow flexibility at G's Academy Fukuoka

RIGHT An ambiguous in-between space like engawa in Japanese architecture is provided in front of the security gate equipped with a smart lock, loosely connecting inside and outside. This project was art directed by MYDO LLC and managed by TRAIL HEADS, Inc. **Photos** Gottingham

FUKUOKA The gentle coolness of Japanese cinema is paired with clean design and trending colours in this mixed-use facility that extends over two floors. The neon sign 'become a geek with the power to change the world' introduces visitors to the programming school G's Academy Fukuoka.

The premise of the operation is to offer a straightforward design for Fukuoka's unique geeks that offers flexible facilities at a reasonable cost, following the Japanese Yatai – small, mobile food stalls that appear in the early evening and disappear again later. Expenditure has been kept to a minimum by using inexpensive materials like industrial steel, plywood and vinyl. While most of the space has been treated to allow for an open-plan setting, compartments can be created using the bright orange curtains present throughout. The design appears robust and straightforward but stems from substantial research of the city of Fukuoka, resulting in a unique visual language.

On the first floor, there is a communal space which is shared by the school and the adjacent co-working space, accommodating an entrance hall, library, kitchen, kiosk, meeting booths, classrooms, workspaces, a multipurpose hall that can be used for various events, utilities including post boxes and lockers. Once pupils finish their engagement with the school, they can benefit directly from the facilities and the professional community inside the co-working space.

The co-working space is where engineers, entrepreneurs and designers can create a dialogue and concentrate on manufacturing

LEFT Inspired by Fukuoka's famous Nakasu food stalls, the kiosk with its mini kitchen naturally attracts people. The components of the industrial workbench were irregularly reconfigured and reconstructed.

RIGHT TOP Classic arm lights, used by drafting technicians and engineers for a long time, look like crab legs.

RIGHT BOTTOM The partition wall system made of a perforated wood board can be customised to meet each user's needs. Classic office chairs made in Japan are used.

The University of Performing Arts Ernst Busch renders visible the process of making theatre through O&O Baukunst's treatment

RIGHT View on the timber-clad fly tower, one of the three main parts of the building.
Photo Horst Stasny

DESIGN FOR INNOVATION

THE UNIVERSITY OF PERFORMING ARTS
ERNST BUSCH

ABOVE The new library is one of the highlights to be enjoyed by the 175 students of the University of Performing Arts Ernst Busch.

RIGHT The raw staircase connects the old elements and the only volumes added where necessary to meet the requirements of a modern theatre school.

NEXT SPREAD The main theatre and event space acts as a black box to be filled with life and reflects the spirit of the city it is housed in, Berlin.
Photos Schnepp Renou

BERLIN The drama school's new location, Ernst Busch, finally unites all the previously scattered facilities. Supplementing the old 1950s building, which used to house the theatre workshops, new components were added to the existing building. The old building was cut open in the front part to insert a tall, timber clad tower which creates a symbol for the academy visible from the street to the entire city.

Two stacked rehearsal stages are located within, also accessible for public performances. The conventionally hidden operations of technical equipment and set are visible from the exterior facade through the veil of a wooden curtain. The illuminated boxiness of the theatre cafe – a glass cube sheathed by a folding perforated metal curtain – joins the existing building to enclose a terrace with outdoor dining on the west side.

The feeling inside the school escapes its technical description; raw concrete and other unfinished materials are an honest and constant ornament. That's the line the architects set up to distinguish old from new and polished from raw. It is an approach that mimics that of making theatre, which is to be imagined like a workshop of constant improvisation, a place where nothing is finished with shining and progress comes from trying each time anew, the pure opposite of 'handling with care' which could be described as 'handling to test' while trusting that the surroundings will be able to withstand repeatedly.

DESIGN FOR INNOVATION

ABOVE Exchange and freedom of expression are emphasised in the building as it is in acting practice.
Photo Harald Hauswald1

RIGHT The encounter between old and new is marked in the interior by a separating line at 2.30 m, extending through the entire building.
Photo Schnepp Renou

The encounter between old and new is shown as a sort of waterline that flows through the building

Practice makes perfect finds an intergenerational application in <u>PPAG architects</u>' Viennese <u>Längenfeldgasse Primary and Vocational School</u>

RIGHT With its six storeys, the building appears high in the Viennese panorama. As little ground area as possible has been used to reserve a sizeable green spot for students.
Photos Hertha Hurnaus

LÄNGENFELDGASSE PRIMARY AND
VOCATIONAL SCHOOL

ABOVE The terraces serve as a meeting place for students of different age groups. In addition, the tubular sports devices provide a recreational function.

RIGHT TOP Playfulness prevails with the creative installation of a large metal slide that can be accessed from and offers an alternative to the external stairs.

RIGHT BOTTOM The school meets all requirements of contemporary teaching thanks to its spatial-pedagogical concept for project-based learning and free appropriation of knowledge. The custom designed storage spaces can easily be reached by children on their own.

NEXT SPREAD The stairs serve as emergency exits and are designed in a way that will be fun for children to use, but is also suitable for teaching outside.

VIENNA A friendly spaceship has arrived in a densely developed area of the city. Six storeys of stainless steel convince of their friendliness with bright yellow, round tubes and corners. A space-saving attitude preserves a large green area for the students of all types.

On the one hand, there are 17 classes of elementary school pupils who inhabit the colourful ground and first floors of the horizontal part of the building. On the other hand, there are 23 classes of vocational students whose space extends in the vertical piece tapering toward the top. The younger children benefit from a cluster system, with four to five educational rooms organised around a learning landscape. Every classroom features an appendix that can be used as a nest or as a quiet space to accommodate different moods and needs. The cluster concept has been adapted for the older students with a 'large multifunctional space and open spaces that operate as points of contact between both institutions. A large terrace above the primary school and staggered terraces connected through external stairs are an integral part of educational space-related considerations.'

These spaces make interconnectivity between the two groups possible while also allowing outside teaching possibilities and visual joy. What makes the school stand out is the conceptual calculation of collaboration between different age groups, thus preparing both groups empathically for the diverse society that awaits them outside the building.

LEFT TOP The yellow highlighting continues from the outside and runs into the indoors, where it gives orientation and freshness in the vocational school. All staircases in the primary school are pink.

LEFT BOTTOM Different graphic patterns and organic shapes are repeated, delivering playfulness and character inside the changing rooms.

RIGHT The gymnasium surprises with a mint green cladding that stimulates the brain while rendering the space more exciting. The natural flow of light and the wooden training devices make for an organic atmosphere.

Inside, mirrors enhance the light
and the outside views, creating
a continuous learning landscape
and a new spatial sensation

This Canadian library network is reinvented by architecture studio <u>RDHA</u> to include creative workshops in the <u>Idea Exchange Old Post Office</u>

RIGHT Sitting on the bank of the Grand River, the project reactivates the listed 1885 masonry post office. In addition, it adds a sizeable transparent pavilion that extends around the original building and over the water, signalling the presence of a new landmark. **Photos** Tom Arban

IDEA EXCHANGE OLD POST OFFICE

ABOVE Adults can familiarise themselves with new technology and printing techniques that they would have difficulty accessing in non-professional contexts.

LEFT The new building is conceived as a glass box entrance that contrasts the restored masonry found in the original building. Lounge areas offer floor-to-ceiling views of the river and its surroundings.

CAMBRIDGE At first, a 'bookless' library does not necessarily seem like an excellent idea to foster education. However, in this case, it must be noted that there is another, more traditional library of 'Idea Exchange'. This rebranding of the Cambridge library network is situated just across the bridge, on the bank of the Grand River, adjacent to the Old Post Office.

The idea is to offer a type of space that presents an innovative opportunity to study and enlarge one's horizon – as would have been the case in libraries before our time. The original building, a masonry post office built in 1885, lends itself perfectly to the pursuit of creativity and has been completed with the addition of an 836-m^2 transparent volume wrapping around it, creating an enticing contrast for visitors and passers-by.

The newly developed digital hub is an intelligent take on adult learning, saving itself from obsolescence while bringing in and educating former bookworms in digital technologies. A whole day can easily be spent here – performance spaces with black box theatre and audio recording equipment are in the basement, while the 'Reading Room Cafe' and restaurant are just above on ground level. On the second level can be found the discovery centre for children, providing robot building kits as well as first encounters with laptops and other digital equipment while opening to a large rooftop terrace. Finally, the exceptional attic becomes the playground for adults with laser-cutting machines, 3D printers, soldering stations, sewing machines and wood and metal tools.

In rural Denmark, Reiulf Ramstad Arkitekter shines a bright light on local tradition with Kornets Hus

ABOVE The austere architecture translates into a remarkable shape that stands out without overshadowing the grain fields in which it is situated.

RIGHT TOP The wood-clad teaching and exhibition spaces are marked by an attention to natural lighting and increased volume of the skylights.

RIGHT BOTTOM The interior has been designed to frame the outward view onto the fields and open up onto the terrace. The public spaces evolve around the central bread oven.

HJØRRING The history of grain and its cultivation is crucial to the history of humankind, with storage and cultivation describing milestones in social progress. As one of the most continental regions in Denmark, the tradition of grain culture and products is even more tangible for the Jutland region, stemming from a deep connection between settlers and the land. The Kornets Hus' mission is to disseminate this rich local food story and farming tradition to newer generations, building on the existing clientele of the farm and bakery, whose land holds the novel inspiration centre.

The building is simple yet distinct, contrasting with the gentle landscape and thus highlighting the fields in which it is immersed. Organised around a simple plan, both the interior and exterior are made of oak, radiating warmth, simplicity and well-known association to Nordic design. As the architects explain, references in architectural form come from 'research into the region's rich landscape, folk culture and agricultural heritage – the centre being defined by its two brick-clad light wells, which reinterpret baker's kilns.' Indeed, the public spaces dedicated to teaching are centred around a large bread oven. Meanwhile, the boundaries between inside and outside are blurred. Light – a source of vital energy for both grain and humans – enters through large windows giving onto the fields.

Teaching and exhibition spaces are demarked by the natural lighting and increased volume of the skylights

Fostering connection becomes the lesson to learn in <u>Basisschool Veerkracht</u>, a protestant-christian primary school designed by <u>Studio Ard Hoksbergen</u> and <u>Studioninedots</u>

RIGHT The classrooms face away from the busy neighbourhood, giving children a sense of intimacy by shading them from the views of passersby.
Photos Milad Pallesh

AMSTERDAM A school carrying the name 'Resilience' is particular for an educational institution, for what is there to be resilient to? The answer seems to be found in the unthought-of everyday pressures. As an example, in the new school, features that didn't work in the old building are no longer present in the design – a schoolyard situated on a busy road, hot classrooms facing south and an elongated building structure. Instead, the lead principles here are safety, challenge and openness.

The section housing the classrooms is disconnected from the main entrance to allow quiet and focused energy in the learning area. Large windows dominate all spaces and internal openings, allowing visual relations between functions so that all attendees – students and teachers alike – are more or less visible to one another, strengthening the sense of community that is so vital for an intimate learning environment fostering comfort and trust. Special attention has been given to sports and exercise facilities that act as a connector on multiple levels. Architecturally, a 5-m folding wall can be opened to transform the gym into an extension of the auditorium. Socially, the gym has been constructed to follow all guidelines for various types of sport. The gym can be rented to sports clubs in the evening, further opening to and enlarging the interaction with the local community.

ABOVE A modern and bright gymnasium with natural light. The space is rented out to sports clubs and other functions to enlarge the community.

RIGHT Playful yet simple hallway with vaulted roof structure that connects all the classrooms.

The design favours as many passive interventions as possible, leading to an energy-efficient, healthy and sustainable school

An ambitious architectural intervention by <u>Woods Bagot</u> connects formerly fragmented sites of study with Melbourne's <u>Deakin Law School Building</u>

DEAKIN LAW SCHOOL BUILDING

LEFT The building has five levels of flexible learning spaces that cut across the continuum of formal class and informal study, with students able to move easily between learning modes.

RIGHT A large, tiered presentation hall has been designed to function as a collaborative space when not in use. This way, large groups can work here when nothing else is scheduled.

MELBOURNE Woods Bagot's Deakin Law School Building introduces a sculptural and monumental learning environment to reconcile the university's splintered Burwood Campus in Melbourne. Providing a point of orientation, the structure's arresting geometry arose from the blend of learning spaces addressing an emerging teaching methodology that goes beyond the traditional lecture theatre.

The building delivers five levels of flexible, media-rich learning spaces that cut across the continuum of formality and informality – students can move freely and seamlessly between learning modes. Technology bars, group pods and separate areas create opportunities for connection, collaboration or private study. Two gardens – the 'Wellness Garden' nestled between buildings and the 'Winter Garden' on the fifth level – are dedicated to student support, health and wellbeing services and provide spaces to retreat and contemplate on campus. Fulfilling a double function, significant, tiered presentation spaces are designed to serve as collaborative spaces when not in formal presentation mode. Set apart from this main rectilinear teaching wing and in an orchestrated contrast of masses, the 'Premier Learning Space' is clad in zinc and articulated as curved organic extrusions. Each response to the site's sloping landscape moves students energetically through the space, spiralling upward to frame a different view of the precinct. Apart from offering new areas, the contemporary campus also acts as a mediator and connector between the buildings with a newly erected link bridge.

Key takeaways

1 Experimenting with shapes, colours and layouts is the first step to arriving at a radically different concept of education. It seems courageous because it is, seeing the long-term impact small physical modifications can have on the development of learners of each age. However, this potential can be harvested by making bold choices in a sector driven by tradition and untimely norms.

2 Newly championed values are digital skills and social demeanours such as communication within groups, vulnerability, expression and experimentation. Strict paradigms are broken by new ways, materials and considerations that connect social spheres and different areas or rooms to give space to varying moods and needs of each user and the environment around them. In short, do something different.

DESIGN

146

FOR
COMMUNITY

147

Atelier XI's Peach Hut redefines the meaning of site-specificity for a vast rural region

RIGHT The cast-in-place concrete miniatures are conceived as a series of invisible arcs derived from the earth and the cloud, culminating in a peachy colour. **Photos** Zhang Chao

ABOVE The large panoramic opening gives onto the vast surrounding land, turning the project into a contemporary cabin.

RIGHT A rounded ceiling and rose-orange glow give comfort to the local community.

NEXT SPREAD Mimicking organic forms as well as brutalist structures, the building holds opposites together in a unique shape.

JIAOZUO 'In the beginning, the architect received the original commission to design a 300-m² public building for facilitating the county's culture and art education in Xiuwu, Henan' – this is how the story starts. A large and extensively functional multipurpose community centre could have been built. Instead, Peach Hut is only one of seven miniature pavilions that will be completed in various locations ranging from fields, woods, lakes and abandoned villages to mountaintops. Splitting the project into seven independent parts is the solution proposed by the architect in response to the vast 630-km² county area that one building should have served in theory, making it thus possible for the residents of these remote rural areas to access the educational resources and make use of the creative communal spaces more efficiently.

The cast-in-place miniatures are made from concrete, mimicking organic shapes that blur the boundaries between outdoor and indoor space by giving specific attention to the light and view. Small and unique spectacles, each is directly inspired by and responding to the site it is on. Divided into two construction phases, the first serves the local community with a vernacular theatre, a beverage bar in a peach tree farmland, and a communal library.

DESIGN FOR COMMUNITY

In the Peach Hut, all windows are diverse shapes, responding to different views and light angles coming from the field

Calujac Architecture's ARTCOR expands the Moldovan Art Academy and creates connections with the outside world

RIGHT Corrugated steel panels and a concrete wall with sculpted details give the quirky structure a visible framing.
Photo Volker Kreidler

ABOVE Steps and seating at the same time. Every inch of space needs to be utilised in a limited setting. A multifunctional room for screenings and gatherings extends over the bottom floor.

LEFT View of the narrow plot which determined the placing and structure of the new building.
Photos Oleg Bajura

CHIȘINĂU The impressive structure of the Creative Industries Center, ARTCOR, emerges from the courtyard of the Moldovan Art Academy in the historical centre of Chișinău. Its mission is to connect young artists with entrepreneurs, media and film producers as well as other creative individuals who want to be integrated into the creative industry.

The existing university building has been connected with the new construction to offer a new space for creative industries within Moldova. Together they form one art hub that combines the multiple design factors to obtain socio-formative freedom and aesthetic expression. While the new building is slightly smaller than the existing academy, it has specific provisions for expositions, performances and workshops. It features a roof terrace with access through the open-air auditorium stairs. The renovated part of the Art Academy's building includes a media library, meeting rooms, a good recording space and rehearsal rooms in the refitted basement. The plan of the new structure follows the lines of the surrounding elements, taking into account already existing viewpoints. As visitors approach, the building gradually opens up, shrinks and expands again across its towering weathering steel composition. The decorative elements for the complex were created, bringing together artists, academy professors and students.

GF Architecture and Paul Mok emphasise the importance of the social sphere at Erdu Primary School

ERDU PRIMARY SCHOOL

No fancy construction materials or details – here, simplicity wins with concrete and stucco

ZHEJIANG As many residents from rural China have migrated to urban areas, the school has experienced a considerable drop of fifty per cent of students. The local government had to respond to this trend innovatively to better accommodate the remaining students, hence adopting small-class-teaching as a potentially more suitable teaching model.

Erdu Primary School is the first pilot project of this kind in rural China. Architecturally speaking, classrooms have been given less space than the conventional school layout. This additional area has become the heart of the school, creating green outdoor pockets, playgrounds and intermittent areas in which socialising can take place across different classes and groups. Apart from curricular activities, the social exchange between groups and individuals is crucial for the primary school experience.

Stimulated here through simple design interventions, such as bright yellow pathways that define familiar places – plazas and playgrounds can be found on the ground floor – and uncomplicated, brilliant indoor facilities, which are further completed by an amphitheatre and a sports complex containing a basketball court and running track. Spaciousness radiates through the extended walkways and gives way to the natural light flooding the various school sections, ultimately making it a pleasurable model for pupils to learn with and from each other.

ERDU PRIMARY SCHOOL

GF ARCHITECTURE AND PAUL MOK

With an intelligent intervention by <u>HUB</u>, minus and minus results in a big plus at <u>Groenendaal College and Park Classrooms</u>

ABOVE View on the castle. The
site is located within a remote part
of the grounds near the pond.
Photo Wouter De Ceuster

RIGHT Royalty is interpreted in
a contemporary manner: high
ceilings, lavishly long curtains
and large amounts of natural light
dominate the entrance area.
Photo David Jacobs

MERKSEM A heritage-listed castle has been transformed into a school,
valorising the building's splendour while facing the difficulties of
imposing changes onto a heritage-listed property. Naturally, the heritage status of the original building didn't allow for drastic changes, and
in addition, the adjacent park features a similar natural-historical value
that excludes the possibility of extending the volume. At the same time,
the view from the historical salons of the castle has been technically
blocked by the addition of an outbuilding in the 1950s, hence becoming
highly problematic as teaching spaces for their lack of natural sunlight
while the outbuilding's 'heavy, concrete structure and low height' have
produced a building that makes a qualitative use of the space unlikely.
A double negation of freedom, so to speak.

Solving the riddle to create additional classrooms and rooms
for a public program despite these and other limitations, the architects
made a significant intervention in the 1950s outbuilding, breaking open
the floor and replacing the solid roof with a glass covering. The result
is an excessive double-height space that allows daylight to flood the
premises and can be used as communal space for various functions,
thus leaving the castle rooms – now reached by sunlight – to be used for
regular school activities.

GROENENDAAL COLLEGE AND PARK
CLASSROOMS

With an inspiring view into the green, the connection between inside and outside has been re-established

LEFT The interiors are kept to an elegant minimum, letting the pupils, the park and castle history on the outside shine.
Photo Wouter De Ceuster

RIGHT TOP The four new classrooms are located within a pavilion with a tilting roofline. The architects determined its position after closely examining the trees on site.
Photo David Jacobs

RIGHT BOTTOM A shared central area can be used as needed and allows children to play freely during downtime.
Photo David Jacobs

GROENENDAAL COLLEGE AND PARK CLASSROOMS

Above the Arctic Circle, the <u>House of Knowledge</u> stands as a radical example of a multifunctional community centre developed by <u>Liljewall</u> and <u>MAF Arkitektkontor</u>

RIGHT The building from above. Paths across the rooftop create a pattern that strengthens the building's identity on digital map services and give a sense of its approximately 23,000 m² with the neighbouring houses. **Photo** Anders Bobert

DESIGN FOR COMMUNITY

GÄLLIVARE Situated north of the Arctic Circle, the necessity for the House of Knowledge is born out of the town of Malmberget having to move due to mining and landslide risk. Merging the city centre, housing and school with the neighbouring Gällivare, the ambitious idea of building a 'world-class Arctic small town' has been established through citizen dialogues and contact with local businesses and other stakeholders. The House of Knowledge is the personification of this ambitious endeavour and a unique opportunity to create a landmark building that is firmly directed to the future while serving to fulfil the everyday needs of its inhabitants.

The six-storey high school has been designed as a marker that tells a story about the culture and the place. The asymmetric shape visually minimises the large-scale complex and lets it take a unique position but not out of place regarding existing buildings in the square. It is a matter of respect and consideration, reflected in the pride that the pupils, teachers and workers feel who use it every day. The community process in which the complex has been built and its mission to be economically, ecologically and socially sustainable gives it its personality and inspires those inside to do their part.

LEFT The meeting point between the new school and its ascendant now accommodates the local museum. The different levels of the facade help the new school fit appropriately into the city.
Photo Anders Bobert

RIGHT The colour of the facade is inspired by the reddest elements to be found in the surrounding Arctic nature. The rooftop is covered by different types of flora especially adapted to this harsh climate.
Photo Anna Kristinsdóttir

NEXT SPREAD It is possible to arrange public exhibitions, performances, and presentations in the entrance hall. Here, a grand staircase is winding from floor to floor. Along the black surface of the steel, different angles are broken into a movement inspired by the tunnels inside a mine. There is also an open fire.
Photo Anders Bobert

DESIGN FOR COMMUNITY

Coming from the reddest elements in nature, the colour makes the building vibrate toward the city and the white snow

LEFT AND ABOVE Some of the furniture in the House of Knowledge is specially conceived. Through its flexible modules system, this bench is easy to combine in different ways. The design connects local traditions, arts, crafts and techniques.
Photos Anders Bobert

RIGHT Common conference premises and an adjoining terrace are situated on the sixth and highest floor. From here you have a spectacular view of the neighbouring mountain called Dundret.
Photo Anna Kristinsdóttir

In OFFICE-UNTITLED's Cayton Children's Museum the power of play is a priority

ABOVE The museum features a non-linear design with various freestanding, tactile objects that unite to five neighbourhoods that children can discover one after the other.

LEFT There is no order or roadmap; children can freely choose where to look first or how long to prevail inside the different installations.

SANTA MONICA The Cayton Children's Museum combines the limitless discovery of play with the designed safety of an indoor space. Extending over 1800 m^2, it was intended as a series of unexpected spaces that inspire children to learn about and engage with their surroundings. The museum is situated on the upper floor of Santa Monica Place, a retail centre initially designed by Frank Gehry in 1980, re-evaluating the former food halls of the complex with a community impact.

The museum's non-linear design features different immersive sites with a diverse network of freestanding, tactile objects and installations. Five exhibit neighbourhoods complete these: 'Launch Your', hands-on space for toddlers to navigate various types of topography while building coordination and confidence, 'Let's Help', a collection of exhibits dedicated to the role of first responders, veterinarians and farm to meal process that enables our food chain, 'Together We', exhibits that promote collaboration and group interaction, 'Reach For', a space to stretch your capacity and abilities in the 'Cloud Climber' and 'Reflect On', a contemplative neighbourhood with exhibits focused on finding new ways to be present and our ability to connect with nature and those we've lost communication with. Using bright colours and wayfinding throughout, the museum uniquely speaks to the youngest learners and offers a stimulating mode to understand the world.

ABOVE All senses are taken into account. Intense colours are combined with highly tactile experiences like a bath of balls or a suspended net that can be climbed.

RIGHT TOP Being tailored to different ages, the museum allows children to discover on their own. The mirror hall can safely spark the curiosity of smaller visitors.

RIGHT BOTTOM Next to play and adventure, there are spaces for group settings and cognitive learning experiences.

An endless stream of colours and shapes invites children to wonder, marvel, and discover the unknown

CAYTON CHILDREN'S MUSEUM

Ola Roald Arkitektur's project, Ydalir School and Kindergarten, roots sustainability deeply into the social fabric

RIGHT The project is built and clad almost entirely in wood construction to fulfil ambitious goals for sustainable design. The Hedmark region of Norway is well known for its local timber production.
Photo Christoffer Imislund

ABOVE Traditional, Nordic ways of building with wood meet the sleek new methods of cross-laminated timber construction.

RIGHT The school generates daytime and nighttime activity and provides spaces where the local community can gather to reinforce the link between the school and the neighbourhood.
Photos Benjamin Astrup Velure

ELVERUM The Ydalir School and Kindergarten are not a standalone project, but an integral part of the new zero-emission neighbourhood in the municipality of Elverum.

Nearly all the construction used is cross-laminated timber, among the most sustainable options for new constructions that benefit from the lowest embedded carbon footprint available on the market. Moreover, its local availability – the Innlandet region is known for its woodlands and local timber production – creates a tangible connection between the environment and its protection.

In this context, it might well be that school's pupils, who are familiarised with global warming and the strategies that lead to its halting, may develop a heightened sensitivity to the issue. This way, they can educate older family members at home, younger siblings and people from other parts of the world where new construction is predominantly made with materials whose production is insanely energy intensive. Indeed, particular focus has been placed on creating these crossover learning possibilities as well as 'social sustainability' in public spaces where young learners and the wider community can easily mingle and partake in cultural activities. These principles of integration and exchange are crucial to the steady progress of every innovative development.

The use of wood as a construction material, cladding and interior surfaces was the primary tool for reducing the project's total carbon footprint

LEFT TOP An earthy red tone is found throughout different areas of the school to provide visual coherency and belonging.

LEFT BOTTOM Organic shapes and colours render the library a comfortable nook to spend time in.

RIGHT The wood-clad atrium provides a tall light channel.
Photos Benjamin Astrup Velure

B612associates and OSK-AR Architecten design Ket & Co, a luxurious school that recalls the royal gold of the Palace of Versailles with a contemporary twist

BRUSSELS The project Ket & Co consists of a primary school completed with a sports hall, a FabLab and an auditorium located in a very densified and vibrant multicultural neighbourhood, Sint-Jans-Molenbeek, near the city centre of Brussels. With this new school building, resulting in the accommodation of 200 additional students, a long-awaited and very much needed increase of school capacity was realised in Brussels. In this sense, the building provides a service where that service is required.

When Pavilion Dufour, the administrative building adjacent to the Palace of Versailles, was refurbished in 2016, the architects used a similar language for the service interventions – a golden and luxurious yet understated, practical, welcoming and transparent design. Understanding schooling as a provision of service to pupils and the wider community is crucial and exceptionally well-articulated in this project. Designed to act as a catalyst for the whole neighbourhood and its residents, Ket & Co facilitates the use of the infrastructure by local residents outside of school hours.

Enlarging its work field, the school can thus drastically increase its added value for the neighbourhood. The actual value therefore lies within the community and the surplus use they can impose on the facilities daily – the school here becomes part of daily life beyond the academic lecture structure, even integrating plots of vegetable gardens.

LEFT The elegant new school building houses 200 students, a long-awaited and much-needed augmentation of school capacity in Brussels.
Photo Luca Beel

RIGHT Broad corridors with daylight are smooth extensions of the classrooms and can be used for multiple functions, such as spontaneous encounters and joint learning.
Photo Timothy Schiettecatte

BELOW The sports hall is intended to reach further and act as a catalyst for the whole neighbourhood and its residents.
Photo Timothy Schiettecatte

Shulin Architecture Design's Mountain House in Mist provides a space where children and the elderly can feel freedom and happiness

ABOVE Nearly completely translucent, the modest house radiates light through the valley and symbolises happiness.

RIGHT A small pond appears below the bottom of the first-floor patio. Rain drops fall from the deck into the pool on rainy days, and visitors can hear the sound inside.

JINHUA The essence of the structure located in an ancient mountain forest in Wuyi County, Jinhua, Zhejiang Province, is pure and simple. Its secret lies in coexistence. First and foremost, the house concurs with the rich, complex and omnipresent nature scattering the old village at different altitudes within the mountain line, separated by dense, ancient forests. Some of the village features are intact, while others have withered with time, like the collapsed old cowshed. We all must coexist with change, and the village has seen much of it. In this new chapter, the book house aims to propose a serene reading space that allows people to settle for a moment.

On the one hand, the project is targeted toward young people and children who have left the mountains for more liveable conditions. On the other hand, it provides a colourful place in which the elderly can escape isolation and feel the happiness of connection and silent coexistence. Held by ten structural columns, the house features a first floor with an overhead semi-outdoor space and a tiny water bar accessible to villagers and passers-by. The second floor houses the books, shelves and areas for quiet reading. A staircase connects this section to the outdoors, thus linking various activities.

There are two back-shaped bookshelves on the second floor, creating a corridor around the patio and the reading space in the middle

ABOVE Children and the elderly can come together in the book room to read and spend time together.

LEFT TOP People can see through the window and watch others reading books on the balcony while seeing the hills and forests far away.

LEFT BOTTOM It was important for the architect to include a patio to make the house more relevant to nature, time and space.

De Zwarte Hond and Studio Nauta design School by a School, a successful negotiation between old and new

RIGHT The school fully integrates with the existing neighbourhood. **Photos** Jordi Huisman

ABOVE In a new integrated child centre in Leeuwarden, primary school Prins Constantijn and children's day care centre Sinne come together under one roof.

LEFT Archaic forms and floor-to-ceiling windows characterise the extension. Concrete beams and bricks relate to the old building without imitating it.

LEEUWARDEN School by a School is a proud example of a past that has adapted to future needs. Constructed in 1929 in the local Amsterdam School style, the building was aesthetically pleasing but increasingly dysfunctional for its users, the number of whom also increased steadily in the past years. A negotiation between protecting an appreciated piece of local heritage and fulfilling the communities' needs resulted in stripping the original building down to its essence while adding an extension that complements it with necessary features.

A light-flooded atrium has become the heart of the recon-figured school and lined all around, circulation spaces suitable for various schooling enhance flexible learning. A birch plywood stair-case doubles the room up as an amphitheatre, connecting the school and providing a space for performances and events. On the outside, the new facades made of prefabricated concrete columns and warmly tinted brick stand out against the original structure. At the same time, the exposed lintels lining windows in the extension recall existing openings and connect to the building's historic fabric.

New and old coexist with a view onto each other: the historic brick wall lends stamina to the new atrium

Key takeaways

DESIGN FOR COMMUNITY

1   The task is to create a container that fosters encounters. It is safe to say that contrasts and diversity seem to make the best conditions for interesting, casual and honest meetings of worlds. This can mean installing a library among agricultural fields to cultivate the land in another sense and activate the sprawling community around it. It nearly always means considering the users to be very young and older, bringing together complementary groups of age to cohabit and learn from each other while protecting the especially elderly from isolation. Often multiple functions are housed under one roof, ensuring that the target group of each activity brings their set of values and experiences to enrich the community.

2   It seems interesting to consider unexpected places for these points of encounter that significantly enhance the more remote locations of the globe inhabited by humans.

DESIGN

206

                   DESIGN WITH NATURE

Biblioteca Padre Charbonneau, a tropical library by Andrade Morettin Arquitetos puts reading into a new light

LEFT By raising the building's volume above the campus' typical low-rise structures, the library acts as a meeting point for the school's community: a centre of convergence.
Photos Andre Scarpa

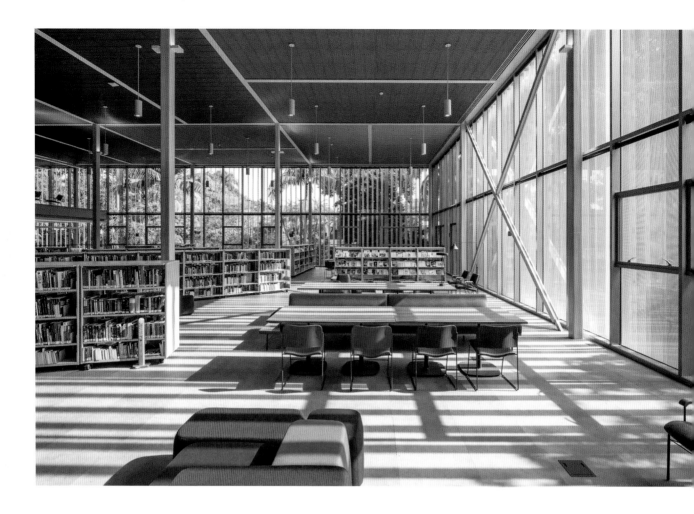

ABOVE The upper volume's double-height ceilings reflect the space's ability to deal with mutable functions and adapt in times of transformations.

RIGHT TOP The elevated volume doubles as a shelter for outdoor spaces, integrating well into the surrounding gardens.

RIGHT BOTTOM Tensioned aluminium sheets line the exterior, acting as a mediator between the interior and exterior spaces and filtering the sunlight.

SÃO PAULO The original library, Colégio Santa Cruz, no longer corresponded to the current demands of the community. The school's facilities, which house students from nursery to high school, are distributed over a vast campus, with many trees in low-rise buildings, no more than 10 m in height.

A central axis connects the two main access streets, which organises the complex. In the centre of this axis, next to the square with its main buildings, is the library. The more reserved activities of the library are housed in the generous volume high above the ground: a free space, double-height, comprehensive and flexible, able to face the mutability of the didactic processes. The enclosure of the suspended volume is composed of two layers. The inner layer, formed predominantly by glass panels, reinforces the desired integration with the school's gardens and ensures abundant natural light for the interior.

The external layer, composed of perforated and tensioned aluminium sheets, acts as a mediator, filtering the light and modulating the relationship between the internal and exterior spaces. Despite the economical and light materials that are also quick to assemble, the structure unites the best of architecture. It is modern and functional without being cold, light-filled and technological, spacious and intimately inviting at the same time.

The construction is composed of a reduced number of industrialised elements

DESIGN WITH NATURE

Get lost in <u>Beeeed Atelier</u>'s romantic time vessel, the <u>Rice Field Bookstore of Tanjiawan Agricultural Site Park</u>

LEFT The sloping roof symbolises rural settlement, defining this public building as being of rural culture.
Photos Lu Weijie

ABOVE The intention was to create an architecture that allows the bookstore to stand out from the surrounding modern high-rises.

RIGHT TOP Inside the building's simple interior, the human body can relax completely to regain the spirit of the rural rice field.

RIGHT BOTTOM Nestled among the golden rice fields, the building is conceived as a milestone connecting the past with the present.

WUZHEN Featuring the time-honoured rice-growing farmland, the Tanjiawan in Wuzhen is regarded as one of the Majiabang cultural sites in the early Neolithic Age in the Taihu Basin on the lower reaches of the Yangtze River. Hence it is a rice field which was cultivated already 6000 years ago. Once the designers learned about this history, they were unable to realise the simple rest pot as initially planned. Together with the client, they considered that the building should lead the visitors to rediscover the history of the land and let them be in awe by it as they oversee the territory.

The idea to integrate a bookstore as the structure's main function came with a twofold reasoning. On the one hand, books have a symbolic value that represents the fusion between past and present, on the other hand, the books also have a practical value for visiting tourists whom they help to learn about and connect with the history of the ancient rice field.

In addition, there is a small exhibition room which houses artefacts and other documents that contextualise the past while looking out onto the field today. As a public building of rural culture, the sloping roof is a symbol of rural settlement. Focusing on the landscape of the countryside, the space covered by the roof pushes people to observe the outside through the glass-steel boundary and broaden their horizon.

Here, the spirit of the rural rice field can be regained

The best of both worlds: <u>Bennington College Commons Renovation</u> keeps its beautiful beaux-arts shell while <u>Christoff: Finio Architecture</u> revolutionises the inside

ABOVE A pedestrian pathway has been cut through the building to connect the two halves of the campus between which it stands.

LEFT Floor-to-ceiling windows on the upper floor co-exist with the original roof.

NEXT SPREAD Creating physical and visual connections between different parts of the campus and, thus, all students has been paramount.

BENNINGTON In the first programmatic update to the original 1932 building, a minor miracle is performed. While a contemporary new entryway on the northern facade is added, a pedestrian pathway is cut through the building to connect the halves of campus it stands between, 16 new classrooms are brought online and dining capacity is doubled, the building's footprint remains the same. A total of nearly 1300 m² of unused space have been reactivated for the new campus learning centre cased in an original Beaux-Arts shell.

'As the original hub of campus activity, Commons was the one building that combined learning, socialising and dining under one roof. Our work restores this spectrum of programming while rejuvenating the spaces and circulation according to contemporary academic, social and architectural contexts,' explain the architects. Therein lies the success of the complex, which radiates an air of modern living spaces through all its interiors, discreet and comfortable. From gender-neutral bathrooms to food preparation services and geothermal energy sources, each element has been reconsidered and brought up to standard to accommodate the needs of learners for decades to come – because an open space for education must start with envisioning the future today.

DESIGN WITH NATURE

LEFT Massive floor-to-ceiling window panels let light in and serve as a mini-break during studying.

RIGHT TOP The renovation also added gathering spaces throughout the building, including a new bookstore, a cafe and bakery and several lounges.

RIGHT BOTTOM An unexpected performance space catapults the new building into the present and towards the future.

Sustainability considerations have guided the renovation process to ensure stable learning conditions for decades to come

With the <u>Park Pavilion, The Hoge Veluwe National Park</u>, the architects <u>De Zwarte Hond</u> and <u>Monadnock</u> imagined a structure that makes a connection with the surrounding landscape

RIGHT Golden hues of a remarkable impact communicate with the natural environment around the building.
Photos Stijn Bollaert

PARK PAVILION, THE HOGE VELUWE
NATIONAL PARK

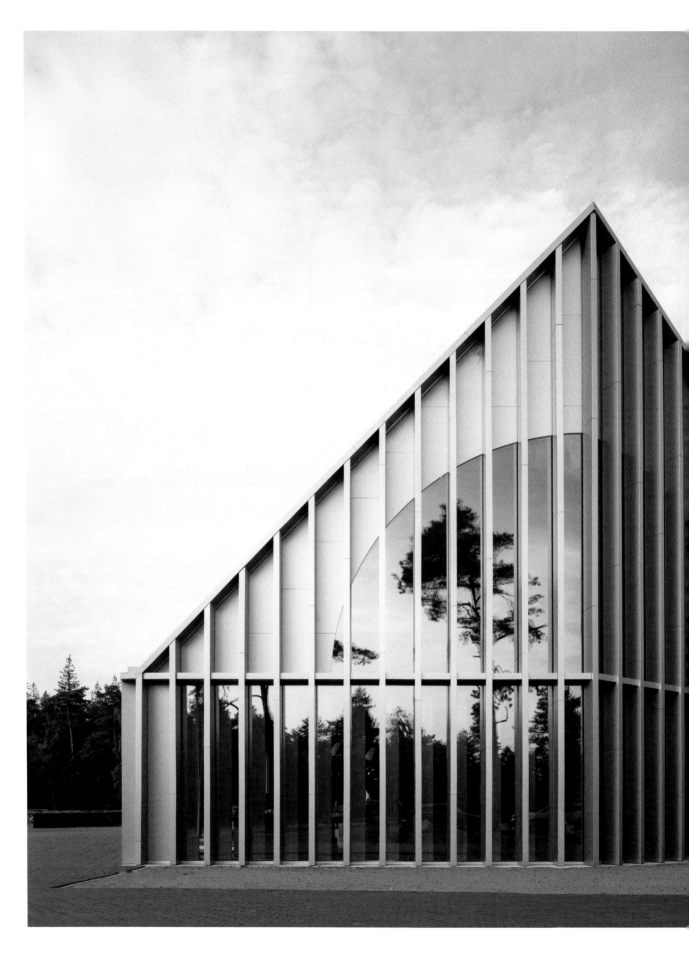

ABOVE Visitors can enjoy the light projections on the vaulted ceiling across the entire elongated and curved central space.

LEFT The entire building reflects the direct connection with the surrounding natural landscape of the Hoge Veluwe.

NEXT SPREAD The large restaurant and learning space feature lampshades with cutouts in organic shapes.

OTTERLO The Hoge Veluwe National Park is a well-hidden gem about 1-hour drive from Amsterdam. The 54-km² nature reserve is also home to the Kröller-Müller Museum, a vast outdoor sculpture park with a noteworthy collection of works. Within this context, the Park Pavilion, on the one hand, needed to become an almost invisible part of the landscape while, on the other, adding an experience to its surroundings. The former request has been fulfilled using organic camouflage techniques like sandstone and wood, together with a large glass facade that spans over the entire length to offer a magnificent view of the majestic forest and grassland. The latter begins with the large 'living room' with a stylish staircase in the centre and a fireplace at the end, all in a contemporary hunting green tone.

The elegant interiors house a shop, a restaurant and educational spaces, ensuring guests can spend the entire day in the park. Above the visitors' heads, nine chandeliers project a magical pattern onto the ceiling, based on an algorithm of the sun shining through the leaves on the vaulted ceiling. Finally, the pavilion's architecture is distinct in style and substantial in size without overpowering the park or sculpture collection, proposing a delicate discourse about the relation between nature and the man-made.

The rustic atmosphere
is enhanced by the use
of natural materials

Drei Architekten's homage to tranquillity, Primary School and Kindergarten in Haslach is a heaven for children

ABOVE All openings in the building are accentuated with white soffits or door frames.

RIGHT The multipurpose hall is used an exercise room for the kindergarten and school as well as for municipal events in the evenings and on weekends.

HASLACH Situated close to the Black Forest, the village of Haslach has retained its traditional charm with half-timbered houses, farm gardens and meadow orchards. The village's school fits into this panorama, and while it imbues the places with contemporary industrialism in steel-grey, it does not dare disturb the idyllic peacefulness. Mimicking a large wooden shed with three gable roofs, the two-storey building offers space for 70 pupils and 20 children for day care. The choice of colours makes this humble yet noticeable appearance possible: 'white plastered walls and ceilings in combination with the warm tone of wooden acoustic elements, panelling or built-in furniture made of silver fir run through all three wings of the building as a connecting element and leave room for colour and liveliness that moves in with the children.'

Rural storage facility on the outside, the inside is dominated by the healthy air of a Swiss sanatorium. Large openings in the facades connect the interior and exterior spaces and flood the building's interior with light, giving a generous spaciousness. The first thing that stands out in the building is the pleasantly restrained choice of materials. This impression is further highlighted by the generous heights, making even single-storey rooms such as the classrooms reach a clear room height of almost 5 m in the ridge area of the roof slope.

PRIMARY SCHOOL AND KINDERGARTEN
IN HASLACH

LEFT Overproportioned hallways operate as flexible learning and lounge areas to connect pupils.

RIGHT TOP Round skylights in transit areas let in natural light and invite pupils to ponder and use them freely as communal spaces.

RIGHT BOTTOM Warm timber cladding extends over the entire interior, lacing the space with intimacy and a protective sphere.

Cognitive performance is improved through David Brownlow Theatre conceived by Jonathan Tuckey Design

RIGHT The wooden construction accentuates the new complex visibly and introduces the concept of sustainability, with wood taking the lead role.
Photo Nick Dearden

NEWTOWN The David Brownlow Theatre was built after the Horris Hill School – a preparatory all-boys institution in a small English village – called for expanding the arts and drama curriculum. The premise for this expansion was that the performing arts improve pupils' confidence, grasp of languages, debating and oratory skills and aptitude.

A modular cabin from the 1970s made way for a new building. Constructed entirely with natural materials, the theatre is passively ventilated. It sits harmoniously within the campus, showing off its cross-laminated timber and wood structural system. This design was chosen for its cost-effectiveness, reasonable construction time and enormous environmental advantage – saving 40 tonnes of CO_2 compared to traditional blockwork.

On the inside, the theatre evokes the pure spirit of a quaker church, echoing the local vernacular in an innovative yet all-encompassing manner. The stage stands out as the only element against the cross-laminated timber frame, wooden benches and grey panelling that covers without ornamentation. The undulating ceiling has been acoustically modelled to project the sound from the stage to the auditorium. Despite not being immediately noticeable, this feature might be the most flamboyant element of the interior design due to its shape and dark blue colour representing the night sky. The architects found inspiration for the project in Christine Boyer's book *The City of Collective Memory*, for its recognition 'that the theatre will be a stage set for everyday life'.

ABOVE The new, sustainable building turned a former car park into a lively place that fits in with the surrounding buildings while being decidedly different. **Photo** Nick Dearden

RIGHT The brick-red colour gives the building a surreal touch without completely distancing it from the organic world, allowing for an exciting contrast with the surrounding vegetation. **Photo** Jim Stephenson

The theatre draws from its surroundings not by replicating the local vernacular, but by being consciously distinct in materiality and structure

RIGHT While theatres and cultural institutions across the UK are being closed, the new theatre will be available to the broader community through local theatre clubs and groups.
Photo Jim Stephenson

BELOW The design resulted from a competition that called for a theatre that could expand the arts and drama curriculum at the school – confirming that performing arts improve confidence, language, debate, oratory and aptitude.
Photo Nick Dearden

An architectural enclave within nature: <u>MU architecture's</u> <u>Media Library Epernon</u> is a destination beyond the expected

BELOW Seemingly floating, the building is raised on stilts to protect it from rising water levels and minimise its impact on its environment. This way, the existing flora and fauna remain intact.

RIGHT TOP Enhancing the flood-prone nature of the place and the marshland landscape, the strong presence of water became a guiding principle of the design.

RIGHT BOTTOM The ceiling stretches out like a canvas onto which artist Raphaelle Ichkinasi expressed the local landscape and heritage of the city of Epernon.

EPERNON Amid the wetlands just west of Paris, a media library has been built into the landscape on a plot between the old town and the new districts. Or, more correctly, onto the landscape. It emerges on stilts so as not to disturb flora and fauna underneath and around. At first, the unavoidable presence of water seemed to be a constraint but gradually appeared as a guiding element for the project.

Conceived as a glass box, even on the inside, the main feature is looking at the tropical outside with its lush green grass and endless panorama, thus the sizeable horizontal roof, the transparent facades and the detached slab further help to eliminate the boundaries between exterior and interior to showcase the biodiversity typical of the region.

The ceiling has been made into a canvas where the artist Raphaelle Ichkinasi has designed a graphic artwork made from the archives of the city of Epernon – referencing local plants and appearing like a reflection of the wetlands. The beautifully designed interior radiates the tranquillity and modernity one would expect from a modern media library, but only through the immense harmony with its surroundings does it turn into an unmissable destination to meet oneself and others.

Learn to look at the outside from <u>Cottonwood Canyon Experience Center</u> designed by <u>Signal Architecture + Research</u>

RIGHT Balancing nature with the manufactured, the Experience Center was designed to suit the landscape it is part of: resilient, rugged and self-sufficient. **Photos** Gabe Border

ABOVE Through thoughtful planning and close attention to prevailing colour schemes, the difference between indoors and outdoors is only lightly conceivable rather than presenting a hard break.

LEFT TOP Metal framing and contemporary features such as sliding doors and large skylights modernise what a barn can be.

LEFT BOTTOM The siding is made of juniper wood, an abundant species in Oregon and naturally resistant to insects and rotting.

WASCO The landscape is essential here, the passing of time marked by the signs that wind and water left on the canyon walls. Cottonwood Canyon State Park was established in 2013 and is Oregon's second-largest state park with over 30 km², a monument to the outdoor experience and a gateway to the natural habitats and wildlife that can only be found in this unfamiliar territory.

The brief for the Cottonwood Canyon Experience Center required a structure that would complement the environment while respecting – instead of comprising – its pristine nature. Hence, the centre is configured to provide shelter from prevailing winds, with immediate openings located on the leeward side of the structure. A juniper shade arbour protects against the direct sun while opposing doors allow for cross-ventilation and translucent roofing welcomes daylight, reducing daytime lighting demands. Further, the sizeable iconic building references the region's typical vernacular architecture, including shaded outdoor space, windbreaks, woodstove hearth and walkways connecting to camping and cabin sites.

The Experience Center serves the community by providing multifunctional spaces for outdoor learning and scenic indoor facilities to host regional activities, environmental education and cultural events for visitors from across Oregon and the surrounding regions.

STAY Architects reimagines the common greenhouse with its curious experimental facility, <u>Glass House Laboratory</u>

RIGHT A glass greenhouse was adopted to combine natural light and ventilation for an artificial growth environment.
Photos Dong-il Lee

ABOVE The space serves to conduct research on the development of herbs, extraction of essential components and the use of the extract.

RIGHT TOP The residential part was finished with wood for insulation and walls made of polycarbonate for external field view.

RIGHT BOTTOM The interior has two storeys. The first floor offers a research space, while the second floor has a relaxation area to observe the entire growing area.

YANGPYEONG-GUN A small-scale greenhouse is an independent space for cultivating plants. In the middle of a quiet residential area among farmland in Yangpyeong-Gun, STAY Architects tried a new interactive growing centre in which cultivation and experimentation are carried out at the same time on the scale of a private greenhouse.

The facilities and exterior of the structure were designed following aeroponic methods of cultivation. As the complex is a hybrid space between laboratory and temporary residence, it is equipped with facilities that allow for various uses. This attempt drew attention from individual owners pursuing business purposes as well as from the younger generation looking for modern agricultural housing as a new prototype of suburban rural life.

To allow for soilless cultivation and research, a glass-type greenhouse was adopted to combine natural light and ventilation with the artificial cultivation method. The greenhouse is divided mainly into a living area and a space for work facilities. To reveal the characteristics of this re-imagined greenhouse – classically a structural building with polycarbonate and linear lighting – galvanised steel and similar materials are used to emphasise the mechanical and laboratory-like feel. The first floor of the living area is a space for research on herbs, while the second floor is a space to rest, observe and analyse the entire greenhouse. Unlike the work area, this study space features rough but warm masonry.

GLASS HOUSE LABORATORY

Between countryside and airport, <u>Zanon Architetti Associati's H-Farm Campus</u> builds the basis for an international future

RIGHT The large campus accommodates children from kindergarten to university. It offers a welcome centre, a student house, a greenhouse for food service, sports fields and a large central community facility with library and meeting spaces.
Photos Marco Zanta

ABOVE Buildings have a maximum of two floors not to impair views of the surrounding countryside. Principles of new rurality have served as a guiding idea for the design.

RIGHT The large windows and transparency within the building leave space to observe the landscape and make the structure appear light despite its remarkable size.

NEXT SPREAD The building is not a separation from nature but a continuation of it, even on the inside.

TREVISO On an area spanning 300,000 m² of land near Venice airport, an ambitious campus has found its articulation between isolated landscape architecture and technologically advanced learning.

The site is home to learners ranging from kindergarten to university. It offers a welcome centre, a student house, a greenhouse for catering, a gymnasium with sports fields and a large central community building comprising a library and meeting spaces. The promoting company aims to train young people by merging the international school system with technologies that can enhance learning experiences.

While the complex is enormous in size, it features simple geometries which leave space for integration within the environment. The concrete structure thus becomes almost invisible against the vastness of its rural context, abandoning any intention of self-referentiality. Large openings such as windows, canopies and open outdoor spaces ensure diversity in visitors' visual field and bring them closer to the admiration of the surrounding nature. The architects' visible strategy was to plant using 'native essences and tree types that can be found in the surrounding countryside and succeed one another creating ever-changing horizons ranging from lawns, grasses, scattered trees and wooded rooms.' Hence, the landscape becomes an educational dimension with which to stimulate new generations to acquire knowledge and respect the territory.

Perforated with nature and landscaping, the complex melts with the environment despite its extraordinary size

Key takeaways

1 A few elements are essential when considering nature as the determining factor of architectural choices. Firstly, the sustainability of materials and their impact on the organic habitat can be no green choice with a negative impact.

2 How does it frame nature and what relation does it establish? Some buildings are simply within nature but demonstrate no respect, no change of perspective, no doubt, no marvel and hence, in the end, nothing but a separation. A structure in nature is not a refuge but a framing device and it is necessary to decide what to frame and how to interact with it.

3 It should be considered what the structure gives to nature. Making no impact is the bare minimum – creating a facility that regenerates and educates is what 'with nature' means.

Designer index

A. Lerman Architects
Tel Aviv, Israel
a-lerman.co.il

A. Lerman Architects is a multi-disciplinary architectural studio located in the downtown area of Tel Aviv. The practice was founded in 2006 by architect Asaf Lerman and is focused on design competitions and public buildings. The practice's portfolio is diverse, ranging from art and cultural institutions to libraries and educational facilities. Unique to the studio is expertise with interventions into concrete brutalist structures, including some of the most prominent and iconic public buildings in Israel.

page 8

a2o architecten
Hasselt and Brussels, Belgium
a2o-architecten.be

a2o is a multidisciplinary team of designers with expertise covering architecture, urban landscaping, interior and spatial transitions. a2o is a breeding ground for innovation seeking to raise the levels of collective value, social engagement and sustainability through their projects. The main office is a co-working space shared with other creative businesses and cultural organisations. With another office in Brussels, the firm is placed in the heart of the dynamic capital of Europe.

page 16

Andrade Morettin Arquitetos
São Paulo, Brazil
andrademorettin.com.br

The office, founded in 1997, emerged from the association of architects Vinicius Andrade and Marcelo Morettin, who both graduated from the School of Architecture and Urbanism at USP. In 2012, Marcelo Maia Rosa and Renata Andrulis joined the firm's partnership. Acting in architecture and urbanism projects, it works with projects of several scales and of quite varied natures, both for the public and private sectors.

page 208

Atelier XI
Jiaozuo, China
atelierxi.com

Founded in 2017 by Xi Chen in New York City, Atelier XI is a design practice currently based in Shenzhen, China. With work focused on public and cultural projects at various scales, the studio is attentive to the needs of diverse groups and scales while aspiring to create spaces that bring unique poetry and profoundness to contemporary urban and rural environments.

page 148

Aurora Arquitectos
Lisbon, Portugal
aurora.com.pt

Founded in 2010 by Sofia Couto and Sérgio Antunes, Aurora Arquitectos was the natural consequence of the joint work developed in the previous years. In its approach, the reaction to the site is significant, what to do with the existing space and elements. Therefore, the challenge is to interpret, scrutinise, copy, distort and even ironise those raw materials, giving them back to the site in a new and unexpected way.

page 24

B612associates
Uccle, Belgium
b612associates.com

B612associates is a Belgian office for contemporary architecture and urban design. The studio's strength is based on a curriculum of engineers and architects, but also a clear understanding of urban planning, philosophy, history and theory of architecture. Those competencies have fostered the architects' ability to capture and translate the essence and quality of each site into compelling projects. Specific needs and constraints of programs constitute the base and the catalysis of B612's reflection.

page 188

Beeeed Atelier
Hangzhou, China
beeeed.cn

Atelier Beeeed was founded in Hangzhou in 2019. The core members of the team have an academic background in architectural design, architectural history, geography, photography, art and other fields. Some members also teach at universities at the same time, forming a working framework in which design and research rely on each other. The studio attaches great importance to the dimensions of 'region' and 'time' and follow these two elements as priorities throughout.

page 212

Calujac Architecture
Chişinău, Moldova
calujac.com

Maxim Calujac, born in 1980, is the founder and the lead architect at Calujac Architecture. The company is engaged in architecture, interior design, urban space design, landscape design and furniture design. Design principles represent the combination of artful details with architectural functionality, which moves effortlessly from the inside to the outside of the buildings conceived.

page 154

Christoff : Finio Architecture
Bennington, VT
christofffinio.com

Founded in 1999, Christoff : Finio
Architecture is a New York-
based architecture and design
studio committed to making
buildings and environments that
bring meaning to a place. Led
by partners Taryn Christoff and
Martin Finio, the studio's projects
are unified by their response to
context, culture and performance
goals. Through an energetic
and interactive process from
conception to completion, C:FA
approaches each project with a
sense of invention and innovation.

page 216

CloudForm Laboratory
Taipei, Taiwan
behance.net/
CloudFormLaboratory

CloudForm Laboratory is a
studio established in 2019. Most
of the projects are designed for
educational spaces. To explore
space-related issues and use
uncommon and unconventional
thinking to carry out design operations, the studio understands
space as a medium to reflect on
the nature of design issues. The
studio's philosophy originates
from the concept that 'clouds
are invisible and intangible.'

page 82

Crossboundaries
Beijing, China
crossboundaries.com

Hao Dong and Binke Lenhardt
founded Crossboundaries in 2005
in Beijing. Today, Crossboundaries
is a multidisciplinary, design-cen-
tred practice with a project portfolio ranging from urban planning,
architecture and interior design
to graphic design, programming,
teaching and event creation.
With a second office in Frankfurt, Germany, Crossboundaries
works with an international team
and practices by name, cross-
ing the boundaries of the design
domain, initiating activities and
dialogues across different fields.

page 28

De Zwarte Hond
Rotterdam, the Netherlands
dezwartehond.nl

De Zwarte Hond is a design
agency for architecture, urban
design and strategy with offices
in Groningen, Rotterdam and
Cologne. Through a combination of social commitment and
craftsmanship, the agency creates projects that are sensitive to
their context, the needs of users
and the vision of the customer.

page 198, 224

Drei Architekten
Stuttgart, Germany
drei-architekten.de

Drei Architekten was founded in 1982 in Stuttgart and has
grown continuously since then.
A team of around 30 architects
carries out feasibility studies,
designs competitions and plans
and implements projects. The
office mainly focuses on public buildings such as schools,
multipurpose halls, residential
and nursing homes, administrative buildings and fire stations.

page 230

Aybars Aşçı (Efficiency
Lab for Architecture)
Brooklyn, USA
efficiencylab.org

'Efficiency is Beautiful' is the
ethos behind Efficiency Lab's re-
search-driven design philosophy
for building a more sustainable,
inclusive and equitable future.
Founded by Aybars Aşçı, the firm
applies first-principles thinking to
every new challenge, combining
conceptual clarity and analyti-
cal processes, including the use
of algorithmic tools and building
performance modelling, to pave
the road toward greater efficiency in the built environment.

page 74

GF Architecture and Paul Mok
Hangzhou, China and
New York, USA
gfarchitecture.com
paul-mok.com

Erdu Primary School was designed by Joe Qiu Jiayu of GF
Architecture and Paul Mok.
Founded in 2002, GF Architecture is now run by Joe Qiu Jiayu.
The office has 20 designers. One
team works on contemporary
architectural and interior design
while the other specialises in
preserving and restoring historic
structures in China. Paul Mok is
a New York-based designer and
visual artist. His recent works
include architecture, furniture for
retail brands and art installations.

page 158

Grafton Architects
Dublin, Ireland
graftonarchitects.ie

Yvonne Farrell and Shelley Mc-
Namara co-founded Grafton Architects in 1978. They run a multidisciplinary practice and have won
numerous awards. In 2020 they
were selected as the Pritzker Prize
Laureates, known internationally
as architecture's highest honour.
In 2018, Yvonne Farrell and Shelley
McNamara were the curators of
the Venice Architecture Biennale.

page 32

HUB
Antwerp, Belgium
hub.eu

Founded in 2004, HUB has since built up a solid reputation with a broad portfolio of projects to make an active contribution to society. Construction – from concept to reality – remains a through-and-through cultural and economic activity for the studio, adding a new layer to the social fabric. Well-designed spaces enable people to lead better lives. They can support a sustainable transition and create opportunities for future generations.

page 162

Jonathan Tuckey Design
London, UK
jonathantuckey.com

Jonathan Tuckey founded the London practice in 2000. Now a team of 23, Jonathan Tuckey Design has garnered an international reputation for working with existing buildings and structures. The studio has expertise in combining contemporary design with layers of built heritage to explore how old and new can coexist and elevate one another. JTD embraces an architecture of change grounded in an acute awareness of style and context.

page 236

Kimmel Eshkolot Architects
Tel Aviv, Israel
Kimmel.co.il

Kimmel Eshkolot Architects is an award-winning Israeli architecture practice founded in 1986 in Tel Aviv by Etan Kimmel and Michal Kimmel Eshkolot. The practice is currently involved in dozens of projects in Israel and Europe, ranging from urban design and public buildings to residential and interior design. Kimmel Eshkolot Architects preserved and rehabilitated Tel Aviv's historic Neve Tzedek neighbourhood in its first years of practice.

page 36

Kokaistudios
Shanghai, China
kokaistudios.com

Kokaistudios is an award-winning architecture and interior design firm founded in 2000 in Venice by Italian architects Filippo Gabbiani and Andrea Destefanis. Headquartered in Shanghai since 2002, it has grown into a firm of 60 people working on a global scale with projects in Asia, the Middle East, Europe and North America. Kokaistudios partners with its clients to collaboratively develop innovative and ground-breaking projects in diverse fields of design.

page 86

ksestudio
Athens, Greece
ksestudio.com

ksestudio is an architecture and design practice based in Athens, led by Sofia Krimizi and Kyriakos Kyriakou. ksestudio operates at the intersection of practice and theory utilizing a variety of formats to address different cultures and audiences in several locations and environments.

page 90

Liljewall
Gothenburg; Stockholm; Malmö, Sweden
liljewall.se

Liljewall is a creative, compassionate and sustainable architectural firm based in Sweden. Founded in 1980 with more than 40 years of experience, the practice currently counts 260 employees with offices in Gothenburg, Stockholm and Malmö. Liljewall creates solutions for everyday spaces in housing, education, sports and leisure, health and care, commercial and industrial projects that make everyday life fun and inviting, functional and effortless.

page 168

MAF Arkitektkontor
Luelå, Sweden
maf-ark.se

MAF is Sweden's second oldest architectural firm. Over the span of eight decades, many private and public projects were completed. The studio is committed to creating meeting places and building communities based on a vision tailored to each project. The practice revolves around clear communication and the sincere desire to listen to the users' needs and goals.

page 168

Max Arkitekter
Stockholm, Sweden
maxarkitekter.se

Max Arkitekter is a small office initially founded in 1978. Today the team consists of six architects with great interest and passion for creating architecture for children and youth. The studio's philosophy is that the architecture of every day should carry with it the magic of the extraordinary. Children are keen observers of their environment and have a sophisticated sense of natural light, materials, colours and spaces.

page 42

META architectuurbureau
Antwerp, Belgium
meta.be

For META, architecture is a craft that requires professional skill: each design problem receives an elaborated solution that doesn't simply mean staying on a well-trodden path. As a designer and builder, META designs a building as perfectly as possible so that its function and usage can be easily adapted. META was founded in 1991, is led by partners Niklaas Deboutte and Eric Soors, and has 15 employees. Their works span all scales of architecture.

page 48

Moguang Studio
Beijing, China
mg-studio.com.cn

Moguang Studio was co-founded by Feng Xin and Li Jiaying in Beijing in 2019. The studio name Moguang implies the unfolding and closing status of a folding fan, which indicates their working and research approach: finding a starting point and extending it to a broader realm that's accurate yet blurred. As a result, the studio's design practices cover various fields, ranging from architecture, landscape and interior to furniture, art exhibitions and more.

page 98

Monadnock
Rotterdam, the Netherlands
monadnock.nl

Monadnock is an architecture practice based in Rotterdam, active in designing, researching, writing and conversing within architecture, urbanism, interior and staging.

page 224

MU architecture
Epernon, France
mu-architecture.fr

Maïra, Ludovic and Grégoire met in 2002 on the campus of the California Polytechnic University. Drawn together by common projects, they founded the agency MU in 2009. From the beginning, the team insisted on the quality of the exchanges between the players of each project and its users. In order to reply to the requirements of the project and to encourage the explorations, MU surrounds itself with numerous partners with a known expertise.

page 242

Nomoto Sekkei
Tokyo, Japan
teppeinomoto.com

Nomoto Sekkei is a Tokyo-based design firm started by Teppei Nomoto in 2011. The firm focuses on designing furniture, spaces and architecture to create a variety of situations and atmospheres. Nomoto Sekkei specialises in clear and practical output by thinking from a fundamental level and coordinating various elements.

page 102

NKBAK
Berlin, Germany
nkbak.de

NKBAK, the studio of Nicole Kerstin Berganski and Andreas Krawczyk, was founded in Frankfurt in 2007. NKBAK's work focuses on questions about different perceptions of space at various scales. The aim is to sensitise people and raise awareness of the living environment beyond the experience of space.

page 54

O&O Baukunst
Berlin, Germany
ortner-ortner.com

O&O Baukunst is led by the architects Roland Duda, Christian Heuchel, Florian Matzker, Markus Penell jointly managed with Laurids Ortner and Manfred Ortner. O&O Baukunst currently has around 70 employees at its three locations in Berlin, Cologne and Vienna. In terms of content, the focus is on European architectural conditions, which must combine historical heritage with the requirements of attractive renewal.

page 110

OFFICEUNTITLED (OU)
Culver City, USA
officeuntitled.com

OFFICEUNTITLED is a curious, energetic American architecture and design firm focused on creative solutions across multiple scales and typologies. Established in 2013 as R&A and rebranded in 2019 as OU, the practice leverages its four principles' award-winning design and project leadership and a broad portfolio of experience in transformative projects. OU sees the value in every project as an opportunity for material and spatial investigation resulting in positive social impact.

page 176

Ola Roald Arkitektur
Oslo and Tønsberg, Norway
olaroald.no

Ola Roald Arkitektur has offices in Oslo and Tønsberg. The studio works closely with clients to ensure a combination of good sustainable architecture and long-term sustainable economy. They have long experience in the use of environmentally friendly materials, and more recently, in the circular economy, where reuse and recycling alternatives are emphasised. In recent years, place development and urban planning have also been an important area of focus for the office.

page 182

OSK-AR architecten
Dilbeek, Belgium
osk-ar.be

OSK-AR is an architecture practice based in Brussels, Belgium. Since its establishment, the office built a portfolio of various scales and typologies within architecture, landscape design and scenography. At OSK-AR, a multidisciplinary team works closely together to produce exciting and appealing architecture that also just works. OSK-AR architecten has been part of various publications and OSK-AR regularly takes part in lectures and debates on innovative educational infrastructure.

page 188

PPAG architects
Vienna, Austria
ppag.at

Anna Popelka and Georg Poduschka established PPAG architects in Vienna, Austria, in 1995. They have since spearheaded projects across many disciplines within architecture, from furniture design to urban planning. Today PPAG has a staff of 20 with offices in Vienna and Berlin. Regardless of the studio's long experience in the field, every project is developed from scratch to ensure the most innovative and best possible solution for every given situation.

page 118

RDHA
Toronto, Ontario
rdharch.com

RDHA is a Toronto-based studio specialising in architecture for the public realm. Founded in 1919, the firm has a wide-ranging body of work, encompassing corporate headquarters, industrial facilities, academic buildings, transportation facilities, recreation centres, libraries, secure buildings and interiors. The firm feels and acts like an emerging design studio, while its legacy provides a solid backbone of technical and managerial experience.

page 126

REDe Architects
Beijing, China
redearchitects.com

REDe Architects is a Beijing-based boutique architecture firm specialising in providing architectural and interior design services for high-end customers from the private and institutional spaces. With a staff of about 20 professionals, the studio delivers highly integrated solutions, starting from architectural planning, interior design, landscape design, all the way to lighting design and accessories to carry out customised design needs.

page 98

Reiulf Ramstad Arkitekter
Oslo, Norway
reiulframstadarkitekter.com

Reiulf Ramstad Arkitekter is an independent architectural firm with a high level of expertise and a distinct ideology. The firm is focused on interlacing a solid conceptual approach with experience from past accomplished projects with offices based in Oslo in Norway and Aarhus in Denmark.

page 130

Rocco Design Architects Associates
Hong Kong, China
rocco.hk

Rocco Design Architects Associates is an architectural practice based in Hong Kong. Working in a region with disparate cultural and physical landscapes, and where values from diverging times and places converge, it believes that architecture is the embodiment of culture – embracing and reinterpreting the past and addressing modernity – and the requirements of contemporary living. As a result, Rocco Design's works are marked by sensitivity and sensibility.

page 60

Shulin Architecture Design
Hangzhou, China
hzshulin.com

Shulin Architecture Design is an architectural design studio that takes the integrated design of architecture, landscape, interior and soft decoration as its main direction. In addition, Shulin takes rural research, the Chinese garden, traditional culture and artistic aesthetics as its ideological source to do independent practical projects and architecture-related research.

page 192

Signal Architecture + Research
Seattle, USA
signalarch.com

Founded by architect Mark Johnson in 2014, Signal Architecture + Research's award-winning structures amplify the stories of place and people through an artful blend of inquiry and architecture. The firm is energised by discovery and collaboration to increase public access to design excellence. Focusing on projects that provide a common good and emphasise the power of location, history and narrative, the firm creates thoughtful architecture that directly responds to communities and the environment.

page 246

STAY Architects
Seoul, South Korea
stayarchitects.com

STAY Architects was established in 2018 by Jung-hee Hong, the head architect, and Justin Ko, the chief director. The studio participates in the entire design process from brand identity to architectural design and strives to create a space where spatiality and personal experience can communicate. It finds this not in visual space but in a synesthetic area that stimulates the imagination.

page 250

Studio Ard Hoksbergen
Amsterdam, the Netherlands
ardhoksbergen.nl

Ard Hoksbergen studied architecture at the Academy of Architecture in Amsterdam, founding his studio in 2012. Since then, he has collaborated on various projects, focusing on medium-sized housing projects and school construction. The integral designs of Studio Ard Hoksbergen are contemporary and timeless at the same time. They are characterised by simplicity and craftsmanship and leave room for the unknown and thus for the future.

page 134

Studio Nauta
Rotterdam, the Netherlands
studionauta.com

Studio Nauta was founded in 2013 in Rotterdam by Jan Nauta. Characterised by a commitment to all scales of architectural design, the work encompasses everything from concept to detail, with making and the craft of architecture deeply woven into the design process. The studio has designed various homes, offices and schools.

page 198

Studioninedots
Amsterdam, the Netherlands
studioninedots.nl

Studioninedots was established in 2011 by Albert Herder, Vincent van der Klei, Arie van der Neut and Metin van Zijl as an architecture and urban design practice whose work extends from housing to urban concepts. The studio excels in projects that create new realities with a sense of place; embracing experiment and spontaneity; catalysing encounters and exchange.

page 134

TEMP
Beijing, China
te-mp.org

TEMP constantly seeks simplicity hidden behind the unpredictable world of different scales: objects, architecture and city. TEMP is an architectural design studio based in Beijing. Founded by Howard Jiho Kim in 2017, TEMP has completed projects in China and Korea and its work has been featured in various international magazines.
page 66

Woods Bagot
Melbourne, Australia
woodsbagot.com

Woods Bagot is a global studio whose services cover design, research, data analytics and consulting to create 'People Architecture'. Celebrating diversity across cultures, free from a signature style, 'People Architecture' is propelled by a shared sense of empathy, where the values of end users and the values of design are the same. Operating from studios in 17 major cities worldwide, Woods Bagot places human experience at the centre of the design process.

page 140

Zanon Architetti Associati
Treviso, Italy
zanonarchitettiassociati.it

Zanon Architetti Associati is an award-winning Italian architectural firm with almost 20 years of experience. The studio was founded in 2006 by architect Mariano Zanon. The range of works includes interventions in all fields of design developed with a sensitive approach to the existing heritage while pursuing the concept of well-being to improve the quality of life.

page 254

Credits

Where We Learn
Reimagining Educational Spaces

Publisher
Frame

Managing Editor
François-Luc Giraldeau

Editorial Assistant
Heidi Macek

Texts
Izabela Anna Rzeczkowska-Moren

Graphic Design
Barbara Iwanicka

Prepress
Edward De Nijs

Cover Photography
Zhang Chao

Printing
IPP Printers

Trade Distribution USA and Canada
ACC Art Books
6 West 18th Street, Suite 4BNYC, NY 10011
E ussales@accartbooks.com
T +1 212 645 1111
F +1 716 242 4811
Books are billed and shipped
by The National Book Network

Trade Distribution Benelux
Van Ditmar Boekenimport B.V.
Herikerbergweg 98
1101 CM Amsterdam-Zuidoost
the Netherlands
T +31 (0)88-1338473
M +31 (0)6-46205118
vanditmar.nl

Trade Distribution Rest of World
Thames & Hudson Ltd
181A High Holborn
London WC1V 7QX
United Kingdom
T +44 20 7845 5000
F +44 20 7845 5050

ISBN: 978-94-92311-58-0

The Koninklijke Bibliotheek lists this publication in the Nederlandse Bibliografie: detailed bibliographic information is available on the internet at http://picarta.pica.nl

Printed on acid-free paper produced from chlorine-free pulp. TCF ∞
Printed in Poland

987654321